The Takeout 25 Effect

Having witnessed many endeavors in the non-profit sector, Parakkat's remarkable journey during the pandemic stands out as a beacon of resilience and innovation. *The Takeout 25 Effect: Mobilizing Community for Positive Change* captures the vital role of community, and the unwavering belief in the power of positive change. This book is a valuable resource for anyone seeking to make a meaningful impact, and I wholeheartedly endorse it as an inspirational guide to the transformative potential of purpose-driven action.
—**Asheesh Advani,** CEO of JA Worldwide and author of *Modern Achievement.* (JA Worldwide is annually ranked as one of the top 10 NGOs in the world and was nominated for the Nobel Peace Prize in 2023.)

The Takeout 25 Effect by Ravi Parakkat highlights community resilience during challenging times and offers a blueprint for civic engagement and economic revival. I witnessed firsthand the extraordinary impact Takeout 25 had on the survival of businesses in River Forest and our neighboring communities in the pandemic's aftermath. This book is a must-read for elected officials and community leaders who will see how the power of community can be harnessed for positive and lasting change.
—**Catherine Adduci,** Village President, River Forest, Illinois, and Past President of Illinois Municipal League

Having triumphed over challenges on the Olympic stage and in my personal journey, I'm thrilled to witness true resilience in action. *The Takeout 25 Effect: Mobilizing Community for Positive Change* exudes the essence of grit, determination, and the limitless power of hope. Parakkat's remarkable talent to not just conquer adversity but transform it into a catalyst for positive change is beyond inspiring. I enthusiastically recommend it as a wellspring of motivation and guidance for those eager to surmount obstacles and create a lasting impact in our world.
—**Chaunte Lowe,** four-time Olympian and American high jump record holder, TedX speaker, cancer survivor and mother of three

This is a book everybody should read. While on one level it is about building a movement to mobilize a community, it is also about the power of ideas, the force of positivity, and the grit to transform challenges into opportunity. It will inspire you to create a movement, however tiny, of your own!
—**Rishad Tobaccowala,** author of *Restoring the Soul of Business: Staying Human in the Age of Data*

The Takeout 25 Effect: Mobilizing Community for Positive Change is a wonderful case study on how simple ideas can make significant change in communities. The creation of this movement, born out of the need to support local restaurants during a seminal point in our global history, will certainly be replicated for so many other different causes. This book offers an excellent roadmap for anyone with an idea of promoting change and sustainability in their own community.
—**Donovan Pepper,** Oak Park resident, civic and business leader, and former director of government relations for the Illinois Restaurant Association and Chicagoland Chamber of Commerce

On the surface, *The Takeout 25 Effect* is a fascinating story about restaurants at a specific time of crisis, but *Takeout 25* is about so much more than that. *Takeout 25* is an inspiring story about how a community can be engaged, united, and organized behind a cause—overcoming countless obstacles and achieving a goal. I often work with communities that are fighting to bring about the change they want to see in their own neighborhoods. They, too, can benefit from the lessons of this book. *Takeout 25* is a blueprint for community mobilization in the current age and empowering others to achieve a shared vision.
—**Bob Tucker,** Chief Operating Officer of the Chicago Community Loan Fund and former Oak Park Village Trustee

Parakkat's story of the Takeout 25 movement, born out of his unwavering belief in the resilience of his community, serves as a beacon of hope and inspiration. I wholeheartedly endorse *The Takeout 25 Effect* as a must-read for anyone seeking inspiration, practical guidance, and a renewed belief in the power of community action.
—**Sheldon Monteiro,** Chief Product Officer, Publicis Sapient

The TAKEOUT 25 Effect

Mobilizing Community for Positive Change

RAVI PARAKKAT

The Takeout 25 Effect: Mobilizing Community for Positive Change

Copyright ©2024 Ravi Parakkat

Published by 20fy LLC

Hardcover ISBN; 979-8-9899195-0-5

Paperback ISBN: 979-8-9899195-1-2

eISBN: 979-8-9899195-2-9

Cover and Interior Design: GKS Creative

Copyediting and Proofreading: Kim Bookless

Project Management: The Cadence Group

All Rights Reserved. No part of this book may be reproduced or transmitted in any form or by any means, electronic or mechanical, including photocopying, recording, or by any information retrieval or storage system, without the prior written consent of the publisher.

I dedicate this book to my Takeout 25 family and to everyone who lost lives, loved ones, and livelihoods during the COVID-19 pandemic.

Thank you Takeout 25 family.

5/13/24

Contents

Foreword xi
Introduction 1

1. **Prelude: Finding Purpose** 3
   Needing More from Life 4
   Pursuing My Purpose 6
   Key Takeaways 9

   PART 1: CREATING A MOVEMENT 11

2. **The Concept: Takeout 25's Birth** 13
   Revisiting October 2020 14
   Mathematics to the Rescue 15
   Communicating and Implementing the Idea 15
   What It Looked Like behind the Scenes 21
   Key Takeaways 25

3. **Growing the Takeout 25 Family** 27
   Growth in Oak Park 29
   The Role of Media 33
   Expansion to Neighboring Communities
      and Beyond 37
   The Communities Served 40
   Key Takeaways 43

4. **Uniting the Business Community 51**
   Why Unite Small Businesses? 52
   Overcoming Initial Challenges 53
   The First In-Person Takeout 25 Owners/Managers
   Meetup 56
   Early Collaborative Initiatives 58
   Key Takeaways 64

5. **Group Administration and Its Moderation 65**
   Upholding the Positivity Rule 66
   The Role of Moderators 69
   Key Takeaways 75

6. **The Significance of Early Events 77**
   Why We Organized Events 80
   Brainstorming and Execution of Event Ideas 82
   Key Takeaways 91

7. **Navigating Politics 93**
   Political Context: National to Local 94
   The Interplay of Personal Politics and Takeout 25 95
   Vaccine Politics and the End of the Pandemic 99
   Key Takeaways 101

PART 2: HARNESSING A MOVEMENT 105

8. **Founding the Not-for-Profit 107**
   Evolving Past the Pandemic 108
   Back to the Drawing Board 109

  Naming the Initiative 110
  Defining the Vision, Mission, and Core Values...........110
  Crafting the Emblem: Logo Design 113
  The Incorporation Process and Board Selection.......115
  Securing Funding and Financial Management..........119
  Introducing Takeout 25 NFP at Barrie Fest..................123
  Key Takeaways..128

9. **Managing a Mission-Aligned Not-for-Profit...... 129**
  Internship Opportunities...131
  Forming Partnerships..134
  Workings of the Takeout 25 Board 138
  Moderators Group and Restaurant
    Owners/Managers Group..139
  Event Coordination...139
  Key Takeaways..141

10. **Essential Initiatives and Their Alignment.......... 143**
  Empowering Local Small Businesses 144
  Tackling Food Insecurity...154
  Commitment to Sustainability 162
  Key Takeaways..181

CONCLUSION:
UNDERSTANDING AND MAGNIFYING THE IMPACT 183

11. **Community Movements and Their**
  Relevance Today.. 185
  Creating Grassroots Movements.....................................186

    Harnessing a Movement 187
    Community Commerce 189
    Relevance in the Age of Amazon and Uber 191

12. External Recognitions Helped
    Gauge Community Impact **193**
    Awards 195
    Case Study 196
    Community Reactions 197

Afterword 209
Acknowledgments 211
Resources 215
About the Author 219

Foreword

Melissa Elsmo
Food Editor for Wednesday Journal
(Growing Community Media)

KETTLESTRINGS, A SCRAPPY LOCAL tavern, opened its doors and started slinging burgers in mid-March 2020. My job as a food writer for *Wednesday Journal*, Oak Park's local newspaper, drew me to the new eatery on opening day. Before I'd even finished the column, however, COVID-19 changed the indoor dining scene, making that bacon jam-topped burger my last dine-in restaurant meal of 2020. Restaurants were plunged into chaos as communities entered mandated lockdowns with strict regulations impacting every aspect of how residents sourced food. The early days of the pandemic challenged just about everyone, but COVID-19 presented an especially harsh set of circumstances for restaurant owners, chefs, waitstaff, and bartenders. As a longtime Oak Park resident, trained chef, and newspaper writer, I was critically aware our beloved establishments were operating on the thinnest of margins long before mandated closures, social distancing, and outdoor dining became an industry-wide reality.

Just as I was becoming increasingly concerned our restaurant community would not be able to withstand a crisis of this magnitude, local debates about the efficacy of mandated dining room closures were becoming louder; outright defiance of statewide mandates was commonplace in some communities I covered for the paper, while others demanded strict adherence to all rules. In Oak Park, some community members began calling out noncompliant restaurants on social media, drawing the attention of the local health department. Simultaneously, owners were desperately trying to keep money coming in by reinventing their dine-in restaurants as carryout establishments. Living through it was stressful. As a writer, it was fascinating. None of it was good for our restaurants. And then Ravi called. A candidate for Oak Park village trustee, Ravi Parakkat reached out in November 2020 to discuss protecting our independent restaurants by creating a pathway to help owners manage the shutdown. He spoke candidly about his frustration around the "very binary debate" that took hold in our community after one local restaurant defied the governor's dining room closure mandate. He was clear we needed to have a solution that was beneficial to both public health and restaurants while helping community members see how making a small commitment could have a meaningful impact on the local economy. He explained simply and clearly by saying, "If we get ten thousand Oak Park households to spend twenty-five dollars each a week or one hundred dollars each a month on local restaurants this winter, then we have the numbers."

At a time when it felt like everyone had differing opinions, it was wildly refreshing to speak with someone seeking solutions that would not only minimize confusion but also help our community rally around fragile restaurants. I was intrigued enough to publish my first story about Takeout 25 in November 2020. The effort was in its infancy, but I knew it had potential as long as the community bought into the math of it all.

Foreword

By December 2020, Takeout 25 had serious momentum. The relentlessly positive Facebook group was gaining more than 1,000 members per week. Their page was filled with photos of the varied dishes people were enjoying after spending their $25 per week. Some images were artfully curated while others featured half-eaten sandwiches and apologies, but all were there to encourage Takeout 25 community members to diversify their tastes and continue making a concerted effort to save our restaurants. There was no doubt about it—people were steadily spending $25 per week on carryout fare.

As enthusiasm grew, Ravi began collaborating with neighboring communities and other media outlets started paying attention to the effort. My second story on Takeout 25, posted less than four weeks after the first, announced the effort was expanding into neighboring River Forest and being replicated in Palo Alto, California, and Queens, New York. Local restaurant owners commented on the "Takeout 25 effect" with several offering quotes to share their appreciation for the Takeout 25 community and their relentless support during difficult days.

Though it was difficult to measure the impact of a $25 per week spend during an unprecedented pandemic, in a little over a month, Takeout 25 had harnessed strength in numbers to make a powerful statement about the importance of local eateries. Sure, some residents questioned Ravi's motivations and others left the group because of strict rules about comments, but overall the relentlessly optimistic group became a much-needed bright spot for thousands of people in Oak Park and beyond. Once the initiative had stabilized, Ravi began uniting restaurant owners behind the scenes, gathering them outside of peak business hours, to create a sense of community in an industry often viewed as competitive and solitary. The owners group worked to create collaborative progressive dinners in the midst of the pandemic. The Taste the Town events supported participating restaurants as well as local nonprofits.

Taste the Town events were a joy to cover—they combined dishes from multiple local restaurants into one delicious experience. Early Taste the Town events were served up drive-thru style, while later iterations were held in person with live music and loads of face-to-face interaction. Each raised significant dollars for local organizations, all while supporting restaurants, minimizing waste, and building community.

As I enjoyed a noteworthy surf and turf cup at the first in-person Taste the Town event in June 2022, I looked around and realized Ravi and his team had successfully brought the virtual world of Takeout 25 to life as supporters enjoyed a meal together for the first time.

In just a couple years and many columns later, Takeout 25 had grown from a simple math equation into a legitimate 501(c)(6) not-for-profit led by an elected Oak Park Village Trustee. I covered the dedication of a bench commissioned by Takeout 25 made from recycled restaurant packaging. I wrote about the organization's commitment to bring ten local vendors to Barrie Fest in Southeast Oak Park—Takeout 25's presence not only increased attendance at the festival but raised dollars for Austin Coming Together based on Chicago's Westside. I listened to Ravi's plan to position Oak Park as a certified green dining hub, encouraged readers to buy Takeout 25 gift card bundles during the holidays, and covered their effort to bring meals to local warming centers in the cold winter. And

Foreword

I was there when he was named among the 2020 Villagers of the Year by *Wednesday Journal*.

Any time Ravi called, I knew a story wasn't far behind. The future of Takeout 25 has yet to be defined, but Ravi's idea to save local restaurants came at a time when our community needed something positive to focus on. In the same way he built connections between restaurants and residents, he built connections inside the restaurant community specifically and the nonprofit community more broadly. He also knew how to connect with local media to both support and challenge his way of thinking. At a time when media had become more polarizing than ever, it was a rare experience to be on the inside of every decision Ravi made as he built Takeout 25. His steadfast commitment and courage to include the local paper in every move Takeout 25 made allowed us to develop a rapport that made my coverage of the initiative between 2020 and 2022 both compelling and impactful.

Introduction

TAKEOUT 25 WAS CREATED as a simple formula to mobilize the community and inject hope into a hopeless situation. To seek a solution that balanced competing interests, in this case the economic survival of restaurants and community public health during a global pandemic. Takeout 25 has been able to bring community members together and support local businesses while also supporting each other through challenging circumstances.

If you are looking to make a difference in people's lives, if you are seeking a more purposeful life, if you want to give back to your community but don't know where to start or how to go about it, then this book is for you. The Takeout 25 journey provides a template for ordinary citizens to give back.

The Takeout 25 journey is also relevant to community leaders, elected officials and people running for local elected office, people involved in or responsible for economic development in their communities, champions of local initiatives that encourage community members to buy/shop local, individuals pursuing social entrepreneurship as a career option, business leaders, students, and entrepreneurs. I sincerely believe that if I can create and harness a movement like Takeout 25, then so can you. It's been the most gratifying and rewarding journey in my life.

In this book, I break down the various elements that contributed to making Takeout 25 an impactful grassroots movement. I start with my personal story, which provides important context for why and how Takeout 25 came to be. The rest of the book—the Takeout 25 story—is divided into two parts:

- Part 1: *Creating a movement.* Here I discuss the birth of Takeout 25, its evolution into a movement, and the factors that contributed to that evolution. I also share the successes and challenges we faced as part of this journey, what we learned from them, and how you can learn from our triumphs and our mistakes.

- Part 2: *Harnessing the movement.* Here I discuss setting up Takeout 25 as a local 501(c)(6) not-for-profit. Once the original mission of helping restaurants survive the pandemic was accomplished, we decided to harness the movement to do more. I guide you through how we expanded the mission and created initiatives aligned with the mission for social impact.

I conclude the book with a framework to share our learnings from the Takeout 25 journey. I walk you through the economic constructs that formed the basis of Takeout 25's success and our vision for the future.

Throughout this book are sprinkled stories that I've collected from community members, volunteers, local restaurants, and partners. I've also included my original posts to the Takeout 25 Facebook group and articles published in the media. These provide real-time perspectives to balance the perspectives and narratives developed in hindsight.

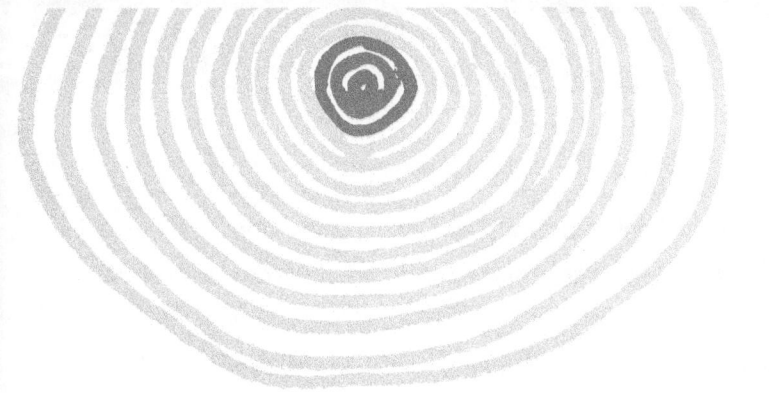

1

Prelude: Finding Purpose

Absolutely amazing what a determined individual can accomplish in his own small circle. A fantastic result during an unprecedented time in our history. You go, Ravi Parakkat and Takeout 25.

—LO ANN

HI, MY NAME IS DAVE, and I am a server at Victory Italian in Oak Park, Illinois. I've been with the company about two years after moving here with my wife from Colorado. She is a proud native of Oak Park! She told me about this group, and being a foodie, I wanted to follow Takeout 25 to get everyone's views on where the best places to eat are. This journey took an unexpected and tragic turn a few months ago when one of our bussers was murdered in a tragic act of domestic violence. Sammy was the sweetest girl ever, maybe my favorite coworker in my twenty-eight years of doing this. I posted her story in the Takeout 25 group, and the outpouring of support was amazing and jaw-dropping to say the least. Many in the group donated money to help her family give her a proper burial and restore the dignity that had been stolen from her. The pain of

losing her will never fade and neither will the kindness community members showed this unknown girl... a few of you reached out to me through Victory Italian to express your condolences, and many others wrote very nice things in the group. My faith in humanity, which had been severely damaged, has been restored. Thank you all for giving me the opportunity to believe that there is good in the world after all.
—**DAVE SCHOMAKER**, server at Victory Italian

Takeout 25 was born out of a combination of my pursuit of a purposeful life and my frustrations about toxic social media conversations that did not result in any meaningful outcomes for the community during a global pandemic.

Needing More from Life

As an engineer and an MBA born and brought up in India, I had spent twenty years as a business consultant solving problems for clients, managing large teams and businesses, and selling advice and solutions to senior leaders in large global corporations. I can't say I was great at all of this, but I had my moments. The learning was great; the money was good. I enjoyed the people I got to meet and work with—most of them, at least. I traveled the world and experienced many cultures and situations. However, after more than fifteen years, this shiny lifestyle started feeling hollow and purposeless.

I became a US citizen in 2016. In the previous decade, my professional focus had evolved from supply chains in manufacturing, to trading and risk management for financial institutions,

Prelude: Finding Purpose

and then to energy (specifically the North American utilities ecosystem). The year 2017 was very successful for me professionally. Among my successes that year, I had worked on conceiving, selling, and piloting a concept to make electricity more affordable to consumers by using technology, data science, and customer engagement. The tangible impact this work had on people's lives, and its potential to scale, struck a chord with me. This initiative convinced me that by using modern technology, data science, and engagement tactics, we could change behaviors to help people reduce their household energy bills. This outcome filled some of the hollowness I was feeling. This, in turn, made me hungry for more work that similarly impacted people's lives. As an employee of a publicly listed company responsible for a book of business, the question I had to grapple with was, Is there enough of this kind of socially impactful work in my portfolio, the North American energy utilities market, to build a viable business? I wanted to believe there was but soon realized this might not be the case.

So, in 2018, I was torn between the need for change and the comfort of the familiar. I was desperately trying to figure out how to take the skills acquired over a twenty-year career in consulting and business management to pursue my purpose—a purpose still vaguely defined, even in my own head.

My response was to make that change happen in a familiar environment. This was the safer and less risky path, or so I thought at the time. This started a yearlong struggle for me to create that new opportunity within the comfort of the organization I had been a part of for thirteen years. I found it tough to balance the commercial pressures of operating a book of business within a listed company with quarterly pressures and my need to create a stream of socially impactful work within this commercial enterprise.

So I moved through 2018 oscillating between my options and still unable to make up my mind. I recall having several clumsy conversations with friends and colleagues. It was no help. In fact, it was excruciatingly painful, and I was finding it difficult to get people to understand me. By the end of 2018, it was clear to me that it was not possible to do what I wanted to do with my employer, and things came to a head in 2019. We agreed that the best option was to part ways, so we did in July 2019.

While expected, it was still a tough period for me. I was letting go of so many things that had shaped my identity to that point. I had also not found anyone who really understood my perspective except for my wife, Amy, who had by then seen me grapple with it for a few years.

Pursuing My Purpose

In 2019, I turned forty-four and found myself in what can only be called a midlife crisis. I had so many obligations and personas to live up to, and that made every decision infinitely more complex. I was still torn between looking back at what I have done in my career and continuing to do that (follow the money and comfort) or look ahead and do what I wanted to do (follow my purpose and the discomfort that comes with the unknown). I spoke to my financial advisor, who assured me I had the financial cushion to take the time to figure things out, and so I did. I decided, very wisely it turns out, to invest time in clarifying my purpose. I had only a vague sense of what I would like to do. I went back to the drawing board and decided it was time for a complete rethink. After weeks of introspection, I was able to articulate my purpose, my values, and how I could pursue my purpose while staying true to my values. The results of my reflections and rethinking were the following: my purpose statement and a set of core values.

My Purpose: Constantly strive to be better than I am today for myself, people around me, and our environment with the goal of impacting a billion lives positively.

Core Values
Personal growth
Relationships
Health
New experiences
Impact

But just writing something down on paper does not change your actions or the trajectory of your life. So I decided to spend my time consistent with my values. I built morning routines and daily schedules to help me with this, and I stuck to them religiously. That turned out to be a great first step, because once I did that, I felt centered and balanced. Now I needed to figure out what direction to take to pursue my purpose.

In early 2020, the world found itself crippled by a global pandemic. I managed to visit India for my nephew's wedding in February 2020. A visit to India always grounds me, and spending time with my large and loving family energizes me. I got back to the US just in time to beat the COVID-related travel restrictions imposed in early March. The next few months were surreal. Schools closed. Remote learning and remote working became the norm. Daily routines were turned on their heads. A global pandemic prompts a lot of existential questions with very few answers.

Then something interesting happened that was a key turning point in my life. In summer 2020, I received a message from a local city council member, Village Trustee Simone Boutet. Simone was planning a run for village president. She had heard about my work as a commissioner at the Oak Park Energy and Environment commission and was reaching out to see whether I would be interested in running for the local village board as a trustee. To say I was surprised would be a gross understatement, but I promised to consider and hung up the phone. I did consider it carefully, and after much thought and discussion, decided I would be able to contribute to my community as it battled the pandemic and the recovery efforts that were sure to follow. It was consistent with my freshly articulated purpose and core values. So, a few weeks later, in August 2020, I called back and agreed to campaign for village trustee. This was the true starting point for the Takeout 25 journey.

I prepared for my campaign and announced my candidacy in October 2020. A political campaign during a pandemic forced me to consume and use social media more than I previously had in my life. I started monitoring local social media groups to get a feel for community issues and priorities. This helped, but soon I got way more than I bargained for.

People were tearing each other down on social media, and it was tearing the community apart. I'm sure this was fueled in part by the pandemic-induced hopelessness and helplessness. The concept of Takeout 25 was born out of the frustration I felt as I observed the toxic tone of the conversations on social media between my fellow community members.

KEY TAKEAWAYS

- While I had heard and read about seeking and pursuing one's purpose, it was really scary for me to go through it.
- Understand your core values. It will help you spend your time well, but be honest with yourself in your self-analysis.
- Place yourself in unfamiliar and uncomfortable situations. It will help you grow in unexpected ways.

PART

Creating a Movement

> Takeout 25 gave the community hope and validated the power of deliberate collective action. While the pandemic is still very much with us it appears that we've had fewer restaurant closings than other communities.
>
> — **DON HARMON**
> (Illinois State Senate President and Oak Park resident)

2

The Concept: Takeout 25's Birth

> *The restaurants in this area are the backbone of social life for the community and a draw that brings others to the area. Sustaining them during the pandemic is a gift to the whole community. Takeout 25 was inspired.*
>
> —VICKY TUFANO

I SAW RAVI'S POST in the Oak Park Dads Facebook group. And that's how it started. Much of the timeline is a blur, as it was for so many of us during the dark time that was COVID. Before I saw Ravi's post, I remember thinking to myself, *This is not going to go well for restaurants.* On November 4, 2020, I made a post about supporting one of my favorite local restaurants. Crickets from the fellow dads, sadly. Little did I know that all it would take was a few people and a shared vision. A short time later, I saw Ravi post his idea for what would soon become Takeout 25 in the very same dads group. So I responded. Trapped at home during lockdown, I was more than happy to use whatever skills I had to support those restaurants that I loved to visit during the "beforetime." Those who were interested met over Zoom and soon formulated a plan that would become

Takeout 25. It's been really cool seeing Takeout 25 grow from just a simple Facebook group of people who loved and cared about their community into something that has actually created more community and helped businesses thrive. Oak Park is a special place in so many ways, and I'm grateful to have been on the ground floor of such a forward-thinking initiative.
—JAYSON FRANKLIN, first volunteer and Takeout 25 Facebook group moderator

Revisiting October 2020

In October 2020, a rise in COVID-19 cases in Illinois prompted a statewide mandate that banned indoor dining at all restaurants. Already the pandemic had pushed restaurants to the brink, and many saw this ordinance as the final nail in the coffin. My favorite breakfast diner, George's, had already invested heavily in plexiglass partitions to make the indoor space safer. George's decided to protest the ordinance by keeping their doors open for indoor dining. This prompted severe community backlash. Many in the community were living in fear with the daily death toll and hospitalization statistics that constantly reminded us of the persistent threat COVID-19 posed. A social media war erupted between those community members who prioritized community health and those who were concerned about the economic survival of their beloved local restaurants. While the pandemic brought out the best in people, it also brought out their worst. I got to observe the negativity and vitriol with no tangible outcomes or meaningful solutions. The two seemingly competing priorities of community health and economic survival of restaurants did not benefit at all from these conversations. In fact, it just tore the community apart and diminished its collective ability to address either issue. I was disgusted by what I saw and decided to seek solutions that could balance community health and restaurant survival.

Mathematics to the Rescue

I started with some basic math and a few assumptions. I worked with publicly and easily available data like local population, the number of restaurants, average household income, etc. It took me a few days to arrive at a simple, meaningful insight: If 10,000 community members spent $25 a week on takeout food, it added up to $1 million in local takeout business each month. This averaged to $10,000 per month for each of the 100 or so local independently owned restaurants in Oak Park. In a community of 55,000, where the average household income is over $93,000 per year, this seemed very achievable. This insight, which I first articulated on October 31, 2020, became Takeout 25.

Communicating and Implementing the Idea

I started to socialize the idea with a group of individuals responsible for economic development in Oak Park. This included the Oak Park Economic Development Corporation, the Oak Park-River Forest Chamber of Commerce, Downtown Oak Park, North Avenue Business District, and leaders from other Oak Park business districts. As time was of the essence, I was expecting/hoping one of these entities would execute the idea. I scheduled a few video calls for the group to get together and figure out how to

THE TAKEOUT 25 EFFECT

best move forward. A couple of calls in, I realized that if this had to happen, then I would have to drive it myself, and so I did.

On November 11, 2020, I posted about the idea on several local Facebook groups and invited volunteers to join this community effort.

> **RAVI'S FACEBOOK POST**
> NOVEMBER 11, 2020
>
> Fellow Oak Parkers,
>
> Ready to spend $25 each week with our local restaurants through this winter? I've done the math (included below if you are interested) and together as a community we can help save the restaurants that form the backbone of our community.
>
> Our restaurants are having to make the difficult choice between community health and economic survival. Without our help, I fear that most will not survive this winter. So please direct your spend locally to help our restaurants.
>
> - Meeting friends or family over Zoom? Order in from the same restaurant and share that experience together.
> - Celebrating a special occasion—Birthday, Anniversary? Consider a local restaurant for takeout.
> - Don't feel like cooking for the holidays? Let a local restaurant help you with that.
>
> This is an urgent need for our restaurants!
>
> Please participate and help spread the word. For listings visit www.carryoutoakpark.com
>
> I'm working closely with OPEDC, OPRF Chamber of Commerce, DTOP, business district leads, a5 Inc., Visit Oak

The Concept: Takeout 25's Birth

> Park, Wednesday Journal, and other business leaders on developing a formal campaign for this. I'm thrilled by how eager and willing these entities are to help our small businesses and to collaborate on this effort to make it happen for Oak Park.
>
> **The Math**
> - ~100 restaurants in Oak Park.
> - Assumed average business subsistence revenue is $10,000 per month (lease, payroll, other bills).
> - We need to mobilize a million dollars a month in restaurant takeout business to get the 100 restaurants $10,000 per month each in revenue.
> - If we get 10,000 Oak Park households to spend $25 each a week/$100 each a month on local restaurants this winter, then we have the numbers.
>
> I understand that there are individuals and families in Oak Park that are struggling and may not be in a position to participate. However, Oak Park has over 22,000 households (52,000 residents) and a median household income of ~$93,000. Finding 10,000 households to spend $25 a week directed locally sounds reasonable. Don't you?

I was thrilled to get pings from Jayson Franklin, Megan Diemer Goodman, and Melanie Sebelka. I invited them to join the next video call I had set up with the business leaders and economic development representatives in our community. In a couple of calls, a subset of the group saw the idea's potential and supported moving forward with it. Now we needed a name for this campaign. With some brainstorming, we came up with names. Carry Out to Carry On, Takeout 25, and Save Our Restaurants were options considered, but we finally selected Takeout 25. It was simple and straightforward, and it represented the idea explicitly. We decided to use the other options as hashtags. In the next seven days, we set up a website, a Facebook group, and a change.org pledge.

I spoke to Melissa Elsmo, the food editor at our local newspaper *Wednesday Journal*, and lined up an article to make the community aware of the launch of Takeout 25. I used this article for my first post in the group.

Introducing: Takeout 25 Oak Park
Pathway to Help Restaurants Manage the Shutdown

by **Melissa Elsmo,** November 18, 2020

This article was originally published in Wednesday Journal and appears here with permission.

Ravi Parakkat, a 14-year Oak Park resident and current village trustee candidate, has pulled together local leaders and residents in an effort to buoy local restaurants through the challenging winter months of COVID-19 ahead.

After witnessing the "very binary debate" generated by one local restaurant's decision to defy the governor's dining room closure mandate, Parakkat went in search of a solution.

"The debate between restaurant survival and public health does not yield any results that benefit the business or broader community," said Parakkat. "The solution has to be beneficial to both."

The Concept: Takeout 25's Birth

Parakkat put his background in consulting and small business ownership to use to create a mathematical formula designed to help community members see how making a small commitment can have a big impact on the local restaurant economy.

There are approximately 100 restaurants in Oak Park, and Parakkat assumed the average basic operating costs for a restaurant is $10,000 per month. That means the Oak Park community must generate a million dollars a month in restaurant takeout business to get the 100 restaurants $10,000 per month in revenue.

Parakkat breaks it down further:

"If we get 10,000 Oak Park households to spend $25 each a week or $100 each a month on local restaurants this winter, then we have the numbers."

Working with the Oak Park Economic Development Corporation, OPRF Chamber of Commerce, Downtown Oak Park, the Hemingway District (and other business district leads), a5 Inc., Visit Oak Park, *Wednesday Journal*, and other leaders in the business community, Parakkat is formalizing a campaign to inspire community members to pledge to spend $25 per week at local restaurants throughout the winter.

The initiative is in its infancy, but you can learn more by visiting takeout25oakpark.com or joining the Takeout 25 Oak Park group on Facebook.

November 17, 2020, was a Tuesday, and our plan was to launch that evening. The launch involved three elements:

- A website to explain the basic Takeout 25 concept to the community (Jayson took the lead on this.)

- A change.org pledge to help community members commit to the $25 a week challenge (Melanie took the lead on this.)
- A public Facebook group to bring community members and local restaurants together and share their dining experiences and photos

The Planning

With the launch date set for November 17, we had a little less than a week to get things in place. I'm so appreciative of those early volunteers like Jayson, Megan, and Melanie, who brought their passion and skills to get us off the ground. The support from John Harris and his team at a5 Inc., a digital marketing agency, was key to us being able to launch on time. The others who were involved in the original brainstorming and planning video calls included Michelle Vanderlaan (local business owner), Judith Alexander (leader of North Avenue District), Shannon Williams (executive director of Downtown Oak Park), Liz Holt and Sam Yousif (OPRF Chamber of Commerce), John Lynch (Oak Park Economic Development Corporation) and Melissa Elsmo (*Wednesday Journal*).

The Pledge

The change.org pledge was a commitment community members had to make as they signed onto the group: a way to increase the sense of accountability to spending $25 per week consistently to support local food businesses. The pledge was useful as we took the early steps, but soon we realized the excitement of meaningful participation to help the community was sufficient motivation for most community members.

The Concept: Takeout 25's Birth

Rules of Engagement
1. **Positivity:** We then discussed the rules of engagement in the group. Based on what I had seen on other local social media groups, I was convinced we needed Takeout 25 to be a positive space. There was much debate and discussion among the local economic development leaders, but I insisted that we adopt a strict positivity rule and make agreeing to that rule a precondition to joining and then staying with the group.
2. **Owners, not awnings:** I was also very particular that it was important for the restaurant owners and staff to participate in the group as people and not as businesses.

So with a simple idea, zero dollars in investment, some volunteer time, a couple of simple rules and guiding principles, and a mountain of hope, we got it all together in time for the launch on November 17. However, we did not start promoting the group until November 18 with the all-important first post. On November 18, 2020, the *Wednesday Journal* article came out, and I used the article for my first post on Takeout 25 Oak Park Facebook group.

What It Looked Like behind the Scenes

So far in this chapter, I have explained how I came up with the idea and the process of giving this idea life. While it may read like a linear path from ideation to action, the truth was far from it. In my head, there was much second-guessing on decisions big and small. Doubts about whether the idea would work, doubts about my ability to execute the idea, doubts about how the community would receive the idea. What kept me going at the time was my conviction that if the idea worked, it would be a lifeline for our small local restaurants. These restaurants make our community livable, and I could not imagine our community being the same in their absence. There was no other solution, nor any other solution providers in sight, to help these small businesses. So the future lay between me attempting this or our local small businesses going unaided.

Centering my actions on a broader purpose to help local restaurants created the external impetus for action. I doubt very much that Takeout 25 would exist if this was not the case. At every step, when I thought of how the presence or absence of this idea in the world could help or hurt lives, I found that my own doubts and insecurities seemed insignificant and melted away. I've used this decision framework for all decisions pertaining to Takeout 25 from then to now, and it's served me well.

Now it was time to actively communicate with the members joining the group.

At the time, I thought early posts were important, and I spent a lot of time thinking about what to post and crafting and refining these messages. It was then I realized that the launch and the initial posts provided a starting point but much more was needed to build an engaged community. Building an engaged community was essential for the idea to work. This was tough enough, but to mobilize the community in a few weeks seemed impossible. It needed a movement!

Within the first few days of its existence, I realized how important it would be to create a consistent "voice of the movement" to communicate with the Takeout 25 community. This is when I started addressing the group as "Dear Takeout 25 family" and used appropriate hashtags like *#saveourrestaurants*, *#carryouttocarryon*, and *#takeout25*. In addition to being consistent, my

The Concept: Takeout 25's Birth

communication with the community needed to be credible and trustworthy. The thing I'm most proud of is that I've been able to build and maintain trust and credibility with the community members as well as restaurant owners and have been very protective of this right from the get-go.

An idea catching on and becoming a movement that mobilizes communities can seem like a matter of luck, a happy happenstance. However, it's a combination of decisions and actions executed with unwavering commitment and laser-focused on purpose. In the following chapters, I'll break down the elements of this journey and the decisions involved, but first let me thank the early believers and volunteers who supported me through those early days.

RAVI'S FACEBOOK POST
DECEMBER 10, 2020

Dear Takeout 25 family,
  I'm overwhelmed by the outpouring of support and encouragement for this initiative. There are a few people that this group needs to know about since their efforts behind the scene have been integral to where we are today.

Jayson Franklin and Melanie Sabelka
Both Jayson and Melanie volunteered to help with the initiative in response to my early reach out on Facebook. Jayson's help with the website and Facebook group is what brought us all together. Melanie helped with the pledge setup and the Google restaurant finder. Thank you, guys. Couldn't have done it without you.

Michelle Vanderlaan and John Harris
Both Michelle and John, as local business leaders, were early believers in the idea, and their marketing savvy and timely advice has really helped me along the way.

Melissa Elsmo
For writing that initial article in WJ that captured the idea so brilliantly in a simple and easy-to-understand way for our community.

Amy Hoffman Parakkat
My wife, who reached out and met as many local restaurants as possible over the last week and spearheaded the PR campaign that got the word out to the media, which was a real game changer. It has been great to share this experience with her.

Last but not least, I have to thank YOU, our community, for joining this movement and inviting your friends and family to join us here. Without broad support from the community, this idea would have been a nonstarter.
Thank you so very much.
I'm so glad that it's working for our local restaurants, and I hope our consistent efforts here will see them through this winter.
I wish I could thank each one of you personally. Thank you all!
#saveourrestaurants
#takeout25oakpark
#carryouttocarryon

The Concept: Takeout 25's Birth

In the next chapter, I'll talk about the growth of the Takeout 25 community—or as I had started by then to address them, *my* Takeout 25 family.

KEY TAKEAWAYS

- Keep the concept simple.
- Ask for help and you shall receive it.
- Money may not be necessary to solve every problem. So do not start with the assumption that it is.
- Self-doubt will occur. Focus on the outcome you want and move forward.
- Do not overthink; just act and evolve.
- Communicate consistently, communicate credibly, and communicate fearlessly. Create a voice for the movement to help with the communication. But most importantly, communicate.

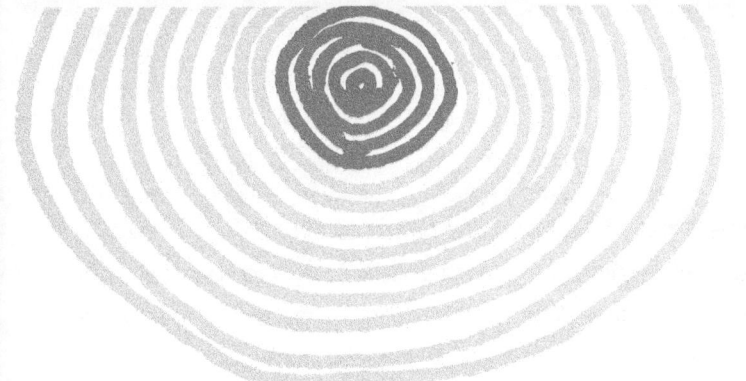

3

Growing the Takeout 25 Family

This unique and pioneering idea allowed thousands of people to spend a modest weekly amount ordering from local restaurants. In the aggregate, dozens and dozens of restaurants survived. It takes a village!

—JIM KELLY

HAVING RETURNED TO THE Chicago area in 2019 after living for eight years elsewhere—California and Brussels, Belgium—and being new transplants to Oak Park, our family was really excited to explore our new home, particularly through dining. My husband and I consider ourselves big foodies, and discovering new restaurants and cuisines by eating (and drinking) out was something that we had enjoyed throughout our relationship, something that helped us to more easily acclimate to our surroundings everywhere in the world, and a beloved pastime that we passed on to our two teenagers. We also loved meeting friends, old and new, over a meal, and we excitedly shared our finds with visiting guests.

THE TAKEOUT 25 EFFECT

It seemed that we had only just begun to explore and grow fond of the many dining options that Oak Park had to offer when the pandemic hit in March 2020. Like so many, the fear of the unknown drove us into our home, and the constant and growing anxiety of becoming seriously ill, or worse, seemed to plague me the most in my family. I felt very isolated and, frankly, was terrified to leave my home. We took solace in having groceries delivered, but cooking all the time quickly got old, and we missed terribly the opportunities to dine out. We gradually began ordering some meals from local restaurants for dining at home, and it gave us a little taste of what we had been missing, but we still didn't have the social aspect of sharing those meals with others. I'm not embarrassed to say that I was suffering emotionally at that time. So, when I learned about Takeout 25 Oak Park and its quest to save our local restaurants by asking residents to commit to spending at least $25/week to takeout/ordering in, it was a no-brainer because we had already met and exceeded that with our family of four. I also appreciated the social network that began to grow within the Takeout 25 Facebook group. I eagerly checked it regularly for updates from neighbors I'd never met, sharing their reviews and photos of meals they'd ordered from their favorite restaurants, some I knew and others that were quickly added to my "Must Try" list. I also loved the sense of community, camaraderie, and positivity with my fellow Oak Parkers, foodies like myself who were united in this common goal of saving our local restaurants, and I was immensely proud that so many in our area were not only surviving but thriving in a climate where all kinds of businesses were closing their doors. Being an avid Facebooker, I also appreciated having an outlet to share my own opinions and

recommendations with others. The group both gave me purpose and made me smile. Since then, Takeout 25 Oak Park has grown and not only enhanced our community through various initiatives but also in other cities, inspiring them to do the same for their local restaurants. I'm immensely proud and fortunate to have witnessed and been part of such an uplifting organization, one that sprang out of a very dark and scary time in the world and in my own life, and which continues to be a positive influence in both. Thank you, Ravi, and thank you, TO25!
—RENEE RUFFIN MERRILL, Oak Park resident

I was convinced that Takeout 25 as a concept could help our local restaurants survive while keeping our community safe from the pandemic. This conviction came with the added pressure for community acceptance of Takeout 25. Acceptance of your idea becomes very important when you believe lives and livelihoods are at stake, and they depend on your idea's success. So, with next to no experience in growing a community on social media, I jumped right in with the zeal of a missionary.

Today we have over 15,000 members. I view this as 15,000 families representing over 30,000 residents in the western suburbs of Chicago.

Growth in Oak Park

The initial focus was to bring the Oak Park community together. My assessment at the time was that there were about 5,000 or so active Facebook users in Oak Park, and I wanted to bring that group together and then use other traditional media channels to get to 10,000 members to make the math work. So, a day after Melissa's introductory article was published, I posted the following:

> **RAVI'S FACEBOOK POST**
> NOVEMBER 19, 2020
>
> Dear Takeout 25 Oak Park members,
>   It's been 24 hours and we are already 315 strong. If each of us get 15 friends to join over the next few days we have 5000 members. That will get us the base required to help our restaurants. I know some of you have already done this but please help invite friends and tap into your local FB groups and network. A few clicks on our phones could change someone's world. Thank you.
> #saveourrestaurants
> #takeout25oakpark
> #carryouttocarryon

The day after the launch, we had more than 100 members; within three days, over 500; and in five days, 1,000 members. I was reaching out to every social media group in town to raise awareness and invite locals to come join the movement, and it was working. I requested folks in my network to invite their local friends and family, and that helped as well. I cannot say with certainty that any one strategy worked better than others, but my approach of trying/exploring every avenue available paid off.

We organically grew at the rate of about 1,000 members a week for the first month. At the time, I was expecting the group to max out at 5,000 members. We crossed that number in five weeks. It took daily posts like the one above and consistent encouragement to get the word out. These five weeks were exhilarating as the concept took off and went viral.

In addition to growing the community to a scale that could make a difference, it was important to me that the community we were building was engaged. I wanted to make sure community members were having a good time once they joined the group. I monitored the group activities relentlessly and was thrilled to see people enthusiastically sharing experiences and having fun interacting with each other on Takeout 25. It provided members some respite from the pandemic isolation. People were posting food pictures and getting excited about local food options. Everyone was discovering new local food establishments to visit and new menu options to consider when they revisited their favorite haunts. The level of engagement in terms of posts, likes, and comments was growing by the minute.

Now the real question was, Was it really helping local restaurants? And if yes, how can we make restaurant owners aware of the idea so they can take full advantage of the opportunity?

The evidence of businesses benefiting from Takeout 25 came when restaurants started offering food specials for Takeout 25 group members and writing thank-you notes to customers referencing the impact Takeout 25 was having on their businesses. Members started posting these messages and offers in the group, which in turn contributed to further engagement and excitement.

THE TAKEOUT 25 EFFECT

A message from a local Italian restaurant, Il Vicolo, on November 24, 2020, was one of the first that referred to Takeout 25 as a movement:

There's a movement going on here in town and we feel its positive vibes. What an awesome platform for all of the local places! We all have a role in this community's success and can't thank you all enough for the constant effort. Food brings us all happiness. It's rewarding when you serve customers and sense the comfort the food has brought over the table. We are so pleased to be able to bring our comfort into your homes as well. Hope we can speak for all the restaurants here in town ... Grazie Oak Park!
—**IL VICOLO**, Oak Park restaurant

Energized by messages like the one above, we doubled down on our efforts to spread the word and involve more restaurants/restaurant owners. Amy, my wife, created flyers, and we dropped them off at local restaurants or handed them to restaurant owners. We spoke to restaurant owners directly every opportunity we got. As I spoke to owners, they would initially look confused, and I would press on. Then their confusion would turn into the realization that this could indeed be helpful, and almost immediately that realization would turn into suspicion. They could not believe that the only expectation was their free participation in this initiative. I realized then that these small business owners were so used to being sold to and taken advantage of that it was hard for them to accept that there was no catch to this idea. They expected Takeout 25 to be a paid service. While participation in Takeout 25 was absolutely free for both the small businesses and community members, these conversations clarified my belief about the concept's intrinsic economic value.

The Role of Media

I'm a big fan of takeout food.

After a long week of work, my wife and I don't want to think about having to cook dinner. We want to change into comfy clothes, sit on the couch with our eight- and six-year-old sons, and enjoy a delicious meal cooked by a great local restaurant. I know many families find themselves in a similar position (plus, no dirty dishes to clean up!). During COVID the local restaurants were still closed and many of them had evolved to a pickup or delivery-only model. As these businesses pivoted, so did our family and we leaned on takeout food more frequently. I'm not sure how I came across a Facebook group called Takeout 25 (or maybe Jenny found it . . . parts of the pandemic have been buried deep in the recesses of my brain), but wow, was this group something. Group members posting pictures of their takeout meals was mouth-watering and we discovered so many local restaurants we never knew existed. It was new. It was exciting. It was an opportunity for our kids to sample a variety of chicken nuggets and fries.

"Hey, look at this picture of the short rib gnocchi from a restaurant on Lake St. It looks incredible."

"We're treating ourselves. Let's order now."

Besides enjoying delicious local food and making our lives easier, we loved the mission of Takeout 25: if every household in our community spent $25 per week on local takeout food, we could

THE TAKEOUT 25 EFFECT

help save the restaurants we loved and the new spots we discovered during this time of social distancing. Math was never my strong suit, but the equation was pretty simple. And, as it turns out, pretty effective.

As the host of a weekly radio show on WGN-AM (720) that focuses on local issues, I wanted to interview the creator of Takeout 25, Ravi Parakkat, because I thought everyone should know about this initiative. Ravi was on a mission to save local businesses and preserve a piece of our culture. And turns out he was just getting started.

Since our first on-air conversation in December of 2020, I have interviewed Ravi six times to date. Over a three-year period, Takeout 25 became a not-for-profit organization and incorporated an emphasis on ending food insecurity and promoting environmental sustainability, all while continuing the original Facebook group that still inspires my takeout adventures to this day.

Takeout 25's reach continues to expand. The organization recently partnered with local restaurants to create the first green dining hub in Illinois. It's caught the attention of the next generation too. My full-time job is teaching history at our local high school, and Takeout 25 was recently invited to our civics volunteer fair. Student interest in the organization was high and many signed up as volunteers.

When innovation, economic hardship, and the love of food intersected, Takeout 25 was born. And man am I glad it was. Now if you'll excuse me, I need to go pick up my sushi order.
—**MIKE STEPHEN**, host of *Outside the Loop* on WGN-AM (720); history teacher, Oak Park and River Forest High School

The media has played a crucial role in helping Takeout 25 reach more people quickly and help the concept spread. Media, along with word of mouth and social media shares, made Takeout 25 into a grassroots movement. For some media outlets, Takeout 25 was a feel-good pandemic story that they wanted to include in their pandemic coverage, while others really saw it as an evolving story that they could cover over time. I viewed all media outlets as partners in this journey. I wanted to provide the media full access to all my decisions relating to Takeout 25 and share the consequences of my decisions with them and the community at large, transparently on a real-time basis.

I've included and quoted some of the published articles in this book. The front-page article in the *Chicago Tribune* written by Steve Johnson and published on May 21, 2021, as Takeout 25 expanded into the Austin neighborhood of Chicago, just to the east of Oak Park, is an example. I've also included the article from Axiom News as part of their regenerative pandemic stories series written by Rachel Kathleen Hindery, published on June 15, 2021.

This also started two relationships that have been integral to the Takeout 25 story to this day: Melissa Elsmo, the food editor of the local newspaper *Wednesday Journal*, and Mike Stephen, host of the WGN radio show *Outside the Loop*.

As I shared in chapter 2, Melissa introduced the Takeout 25 concept to the community with the article "Introducing Takeout 25," and over the past three years, she has written over twenty articles about Takeout 25's evolution.

Mike Stephen, a resident of Oak Park who is a teacher at the local high school and also the host of the WGN radio show *Outside the Loop*, joined the Takeout 25 group shortly after its launch. He reached out to me in December 2020, a month after Takeout 25 was launched, requesting an interview. I said yes without hesitation. That first conversation led to six more interviews over the next couple of years. What Melissa did in print, Mike did on radio. Together, they have chronicled crucial events in Takeout 25's evolution. These partnerships have evolved into friendships, and for this I'm truly grateful.

In December 2020, winter was looming, and we wanted the Takeout 25 concept to spread so more restaurants in more places could survive the COVID-19 winter. Anna Davlantes's show on WGN radio reached out to me for an interview on December 10, 2020. This interview helped get the word out to the greater Chicagoland area. Amy, my wife, reached out to some of the TV channels, and NBC and Fox decided to cover the story in their evening news segment. Chris Coffey from NBC 5 and Brittany Grazillo from Fox 32 came down to Oak Park to film the news segments. This coverage prompted several individuals and groups to reach out to me to see if they could borrow the idea for their communities. I said yes to everyone who reached out and tried to help them the best I could. This resulted in the Takeout 25 concept being implemented in Sunnyside, New York; East Palo Alto, California; South Bend, Indiana; and several other US communities. Locally, communities in the greater Chicagoland area like Elmhurst, Villa Park, Naperville, and Evanston also started similar groups. It was then that I started a Messenger group called Takeout 25 Nation to help support all these communities. While I wanted to help these individuals implement Takeout 25 in their communities, my focus remained on Oak Park and its neighboring communities.

Expansion to Neighboring Communities and Beyond

NBC 5 and Fox news (local TV stations) deciding to cover Takeout 25 helped get the word out to communities well beyond Oak Park. They came to Oak Park and interviewed me, other community members, and some local restaurant owners who were all beneficiaries of the Takeout 25 effect. Each restaurant was experiencing a 20-30% increase in sales as a direct result of Takeout 25.

It was then that I met Jimmy Chen, an extremely savvy local business owner who was hesitant to appear on television because of his discomfort with the English language. In my first conversation with Jimmy, I quickly realized his clarity of thought more than made up for his struggle expressing himself in English. That conversation with Jimmy helped me understand Takeout 25 from a small business owner's perspective. He said, "Hey, Ravi, the stimulus money I received from the government is helpful, but it is a one-time shot that you quickly use up in your business. However, what you have done with Takeout 25 is to give me new customers [and hence, revenue streams] that will stay with me well beyond the pandemic."

There were also so many individuals in the community who went above and beyond to invite local friends and family. One that sticks out in my memory and I'm genuinely appreciative of is April Moon, a local real estate agent who was an early believer and supporter. What April said about Takeout 25 and me and how she said it will always remain one of those moments where I felt included in the community that was now home. As an immigrant born and brought up on the other side of the planet, this was important for me.

"If you don't know what Takeout 25 has done for our community and our restaurants, you need to take a moment to read about it. Takeout 25 helped save our restaurants during the pandemic and more importantly brought a community together when we needed it most. Ravi Parakkat came up with a brilliant idea to help our beloved businesses when they needed it the most. I've lived in Oak Park since 1957. My dad was born here in 1918. This is one of the reasons Oak Park is so very special . . . the people. You are one of those special people, Ravi."

It was about the same time that neighboring communities around Oak Park started to express interest in formally joining Takeout 25. Some made the request, while I reached out to the others as part of a conscious decision to build out the footprint of Takeout 25 over a five-mile radius around Oak Park. This raised concerns in the Facebook group about which communities should be a part of Takeout 25.

RAVI'S FACEBOOK POST

DECEMBER 7, 2020

Dear Takeout 25 family,

　The question about who is included on Takeout 25 has come up a few times on the group and also as personal messages to me. And unfortunately I've had to remove a few threads on the group to avoid folks leaving with the wrong impression. I'll try to be as clear as possible here.

　While Takeout 25 was started with Oak Park as the focus, the north side of North Avenue and south side of Roosevelt Road

Growing the Takeout 25 Family

> were always a part of the original scope. Since then we have formally included the River Forest community. The Forest Park community has not formally joined Takeout 25, but I've initiated some conversations and would like to build a mutually beneficial relationship with Forest Park as well (i.e., see Forest Park residents participate in the group and the Forest Park restaurants benefit from the efforts here). I see some organic activity already that includes FP restaurants on the group, which is great.
>
> Ultimately this is about helping restaurants survive this winter, and I do not want strict rules and boundaries to get in the way of great outcomes and impact.
>
> If anyone has questions on this please feel free to PM me for clarification, and I request you to not use the group to debate this point.
>
> Thank you.
>
> #saveourrestaurants

Oak Park was still the core, but River Forest, Forest Park, Berwyn, Austin/Galewood, and Elmwood Park all formally joined Takeout 25. Collectively, this represented a population of over 250,000 and included 200+ local independently owned brick-and-mortar restaurants. This made sense, as it gave residents more choice and variety in dining experience. For the local restaurants, it reflected well over 95% of their current customer base. Increased visibility in neighboring communities would increase the customer base and fuel future growth for restaurants.

THE TAKEOUT 25 EFFECT

> **RAVI'S FACEBOOK POST**
> NOVEMBER 30, 2020
>
> Dear Takeout 25 members,
>
> I'm excited to welcome the River Forest community to Takeout 25. I had a great conversation with Cathy Adduci (River Forest Village President) on Friday, Nov 27, and we agreed that River Forest with its 10,000+ residents and 10 local restaurants would be a great addition to the Takeout 25 family.
>
> We've already added the River Forest restaurants to our listings on the Takeout 25 website (do check them out). The River Forest team has started reaching out to the community about Takeout 25, and their formal community newsletter is expected to carry the details about Takeout 25 this Thursday.
>
> In the meantime, please invite your River Forest friends to join us here, order in, share your orders here, and create a bigger impact for our local restaurants.
>
> #saveourrestaurants
>
> #takeout25oakpark
>
> #carryouttocarryon

The Communities Served

Takeout 25 started with an exclusive focus on Oak Park. However, as described in this chapter, we quickly expanded to include Oak Park's neighboring communities.

Oak Park is the first suburb west of the city of Chicago. Oak Park is known for the architectural legacy of Frank Lloyd Wright and as the birthplace of author Ernst Hemingway and actor Betty White. Its role in racial integration during the 1970s has continued to inspire many to this day. It offers an affluent, diverse, and livable community representative of what the broader American society can be. Its location plays an important role in its desirability and its socio-economic mix. To its east is the Austin neighborhood of Chicago, a predominantly Black neighborhood characterized by poverty, crime, and underinvestment. To Oak Park's west is the predominantly white and affluent bedroom community of River Forest. Also west of Oak Park is Forest Park, a little less affluent than River Forest but with a lively and social business district. To Oak Park's south lies the predominantly Hispanic and business-dense Berwyn. To Oak Park's north are Elmwood Park and Galewood, which is a part of Chicago's Austin neighborhood.

This mix of neighboring communities and its own history sets up Oak Park to be a racially and economically diverse community. Experiments in Oak Park take on a national significance since many of the issues our nation faces are represented in Oak Park.

When Takeout 25 started in Oak Park, the appeal to participate in this movement extended beyond Oak Park's borders to these key neighbors. Bringing consumers together is one thing, but getting small business owners to collaborate is a very different matter.

As former Oak Park Village Trustee Ray Johnson said, "This initiative scaled up across the country, in locals large and small! Cheers to Oak Park, Illinois, for leading the effort."

In the next chapter, I'll talk more about building the owners group.

THE TAKEOUT 25 EFFECT

One of my favorite Takeout 25 memories occurred on December 20, 2022. Like many in health care, my doctor and her staff had been working tirelessly for months helping people affected by the COVID-19 pandemic. My husband and I wanted to do something to show appreciation. This memory involves her office, my favorite Takeout, and the broader Takeout 25 community. It's a small thing but . . . This was my post:

A holiday treat idea! I love my doctor and wanted to bring her and her staff lunch at Lake Street Family Physicians. Ordered three dozen falafel with tahini and pita. Got to see our friend Mohammed, the owner, and start their day with a nice order. When we brought this amazing-smelling food to the doctor's office, the staff was so excited. Fun to take care of our trusted friends in health care and support wonderful local businesses like Jerusalem Cafe. Thanks, Mohammed.

It was an incredibly small thing to do but in the spirit of Takeout 25, sharing with the community made it special. The post got over 120 likes and so many comments about how many people also loved their own doctor in this physician group and how important this medical team is to our community. Equally, there were comments on how people truly loved the food Mohammad and his staff make, and how they, too, support him during this time. Lastly, posts mentioned this small gesture gave them ideas on how they could help others with Takeout. It was a truly a feel good/appreciation fest. The pandemic was hard, but sharing small things we found we could do to help others was invaluable. The shares on Takeout 25 allow us to amplify and build our spirit for win-win outcomes in taking care of ourselves and each other. Thank you for this.

—**DIANE WILSON**, *Oak Park resident*

KEY TAKEAWAYS

- Vision can be broad, but ideas that become movements must be simple and specific. An idea can inspire, energize, and mobilize people when it is easily understood and triggers achievable action.

- Ideas should connect people to causes bigger than themselves. It should convince them that they can be part of the solution.

- Ideas can cross borders and boundaries to bring people together.

- Traditional media in all forms (print, radio, and TV) can be powerful allies and can complement your social media strategy.

Takeout 25 Has Saved Local Restaurants in Oak Park

Now It's Flexing Its Spending Muscle across the Chicago Border, in Austin

by **Steve Johnson** for *Chicago Tribune*, May 13, 2021

As the COVID-19 pandemic dragged on last fall, Ravi Parakkat watched tensions rise in his community between restaurant owners desperate for revenue and officials trying to keep people from congregating indoors.

A potential solution hit him: Why not formalize the idea of ordering takeout, something people were doing already, and turn it into not only a means to a meal but a kind of civic salvation?

"There were lots of 'shop local' initiatives that were going on," Parakkat said. "But even with people spending money, they were not sure whether they were actually contributing to the local economy meaningfully. So this became a very specific ask."

He launched Takeout 25 Oak Park, founded on sweat equity and some simple math: If enough people would commit to spending $25 weekly on to-go dining, labeled the "Carry Out to Carry On pledge," they could keep local restaurants alive.

"We set up a website and the Facebook group. And it also got support from the local newspaper," he said. "And then within a week, we had more than 1,000 people. And in a couple of months, we were at 7,000."

This calorie-based booster club has been a runaway success. Back-of-the-envelope calculations by Parakkat,

Growing the Takeout 25 Family

an engineer, business consultant and, now, newly elected member of the Oak Park Village Board, suggest people participating in the ad hoc program have spent some $3 million on dining in the last handful of months.

Publicity and word-of-mouth led to localized versions of the readily shared, not-for-profit concept springing up around Chicagoland, including in Elmhurst and Villa Park, and the nation, from Palo Alto, California, to Sunnyside, Queens, in New York City.

And now Takeout 25 is taking perhaps its boldest step yet, at least for an Oak Park community that is sometimes reluctant to visit the Chicago neighborhood immediately to the east, across Austin Boulevard.

"Just cross the street," said Malcolm Crawford, executive director of the Austin African American Business Networking Association, the group Parakkat partnered with this month to bring Takeout 25 Oak Park and its spending muscle to the restaurants of Austin. "You don't have to prepare to go across the street."

To some degree Oak Parkers were already doing that, Parakkat said he noticed in the thriving chatter on the Takeout 25 Facebook page.

"I've observed on Takeout 25 how wildly popular Austin eateries like Chubby's Char House & Chef Daddy's are already with Oak Parkers," he wrote in his post on the page announcing the connection. "This partnership formalizes these natural synergies."

So joining the Takeout 25 list—and to the page's vibrant conversation about where to go to get a good version of, say, vegetarian tacos or smoked brisket—are Austin's roughly 50 restaurants, including the likes of Ben's BBQ, the Madison Street soul food mainstay MacArthur's Restaurant, and the

THE TAKEOUT 25 EFFECT

newcomer Chubby's, aiming for an elevated, fresh-made take on traditional fast foods.

"It's great. That's fantastic," said Prentiss Harris, a co-owner of Chubby's, 5963 W. Madison St., still in a soft-open phase that began in January. "What happens is a lot of people eat at Oak Park restaurants that stay in Chicago, and vice versa. It kind of bridges the gap in between, to let people know there's more options out there."

"It's really exciting," said Christy Bonstell, a longtime Oak Parker who has become an avid Takeout 25 participant. "It is really frustrating for me that we are neighbors and it doesn't seem like there's a great deal of interaction. So it seems this will be a good reason to get to know our neighbors."

Plus, it's food.

"I don't think anything brings people together more than food does," she said. "It's such a great conversation starter and thing for people to get excited about. I'm really glad (Parakkat) has decided to do that."

There has been considerable flow between the communities, historically and present day. Much of Austin's housing stock is similar to Oak Park's, and when "white flight" hit Austin in the 1960s, many families relocated to Oak Park, comparatively prosperous and, now, demographically diverse.

Harris says he and Techa Lewis, his fiancée and Chubby's co-owner, live in Oak Park. Crawford, from the Austin business group, raised his kids in Oak Park before moving to Austin. "I always said, I slept in Oak Park, but I lived in Austin. And now I sleep in Austin, and I live in Austin," Crawford said.

But the money has mostly been flowing from east to west, especially to Oak Park's grocery stores. Parakkat and

Growing the Takeout 25 Family

Crawford cite survey statistics asserting that more than 80% of disposable income in Austin ends up in Oak Park.

"How do you have 52,000 people (in Oak Park), and you have seven full-fledged grocery stores," Campbell asks, "and you have Austin, 100,000 people, and we don't have one?"

"So I see Takeout 25 as a way to kind of help to have a reverse flow of people coming to spend money in Austin as these businesses are developed."

Crawford and Parakkat met recently at the corner of Austin Boulevard and Chicago Avenue to have a picture taken. The session turned into a walk east along Chicago, where Crawford, also a building owner, talked of his work to get the street's westernmost stretch, beginning at Cicero Avenue, designated the Soul City Corridor, a cultural mecca along the lines of Chinatown or Greektown.

A key component, he says, will be restaurants. A sign on one Chicago Avenue building says that Batter & Berries, a West Side outpost of the Black-owned Lincoln Park breakfast and lunch favorite, is planning to open there. And the Facebook page for Brown's Soul Food Restaurant says it will reopen soon in its new Chicago Avenue location, a couple of blocks east of Austin Boulevard.

"It's amazing that all the things that we couldn't get people to do, we're getting them to do around food," said Crawford. "Have you seen, on Facebook, how many people were so excited and saying, 'Yes, I can't wait. Let's participate.'?"

Positivity is one of the Takeout 25 guiding principles. Unlike other food-based online communities, it is not a place to complain about portion size or seasonings, Parakkat said, an ethos that now, after some early policing, seems to be ingrained.

He is also pretty confident that, although Takeout 25 was a specific pandemic response, the community will outlast the worst of COVID-19's virulence.

"It will continue. The frame will change from survival to helping the local economy thrive," said Parakkat, who acknowledges that his April Village Board win, with the most votes in a field of six people vying for three seats, was profoundly helped by the Takeout 25 "name recognition" and demonstration "that I have the community's best interests in mind."

Similarly, the impact on some restaurants has been huge.

"It's really changed the whole situation, at least to me and many restaurants I know in the Oak Park area," said Jimmy Chen, owner of the area's Poke Burrito chain, including a store in Oak Park. "Pretty much we were at the moment that we didn't have any hope. Suddenly it happened pretty much overnight. One Thursday night our business almost got back to normal."

This was in early November. He quickly figured out that the then-new Takeout 25 was the driver, and he became a participant in the Facebook community.

"From that point on, our business kept increasing," said Chen, noting Takeout 25 has been better than any stimulus program. "I had to hire more people. We've surpassed what we did before."

At Surf's Up, an area seafood chain with its home store on the northern border of Oak Park, Takeout 25 brought new business in a tough time — and also just awareness of the place, said owner Denise Roy.

"At one point, we were on the brink of closing. It was bad," she said. "(Takeout 25) works because the community

Growing the Takeout 25 Family

just didn't want to see any more restaurants closed. It's really a support group."

And she's been there to pay it forward, welcoming the new Austin additions. She was at Chubby's Char House the day it opened, she said, and looks forward to the Oak Park food community turning its attention to the east.

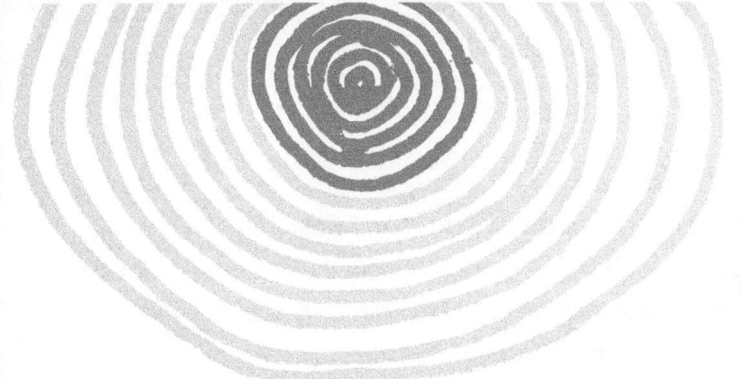

4

Uniting the Business Community

Takeout 25, what an incredible idea! Helping local businesses by encouraging a community to work together. I've learned so much about area businesses I hadn't heard of, about the owners and staff of local restaurants and their struggles during the pandemic. They are my friends now, not just business owners. When I visit, I talk with them, not just order food. The local atmosphere has changed to one of intense caring. I hope the concept spreads far and wide.

—SUE SMALHEISER

THERE ARE ENDLESS WORDS I can say about Takeout 25 and the past three years. I believe the past three years, not only for me but everyone else, have been life-changing experiences. What I can say is that Takeout 25 brought our local businesses together and all the businesses join the journey of helping each other. Without Takeout 25, I couldn't imagine where I would be. We are in the twenty-first century with AI technology and robots, not expecting a pandemic. Never thinking about human relationships. In Oak Park, as a brick-and-mortar small business owner, we got support from our community. I can say our community saved us. Pre-COVID we only focused on doing our own job in our little restaurant and never involved anything

outside of our restaurant. We didn't know our neighbors or other businesses around us. Takeout 25 taught us we have to help each other. We now participate in many community events because we are part of this wonderful community. Without community support, we can't be where we are today. I know many other businesses just like us that need help. We want to help in our community.
—JIMMY CHEN, owner, Poke Burrito

Why Unite Small Businesses?

I knew from the start that bringing local businesses together would be very important and impactful. This idea was further reinforced as I watched restaurant owner Jimmy Chen go around eating at and promoting other restaurants—not just his own!—in the community. Jimmy's posts helped me understand the power of mutual support. His posts gave the restaurants he was posting about a boost, and it was also helping the Takeout 25 community to understand and support Jimmy and his local business, Poke Burrito. However, the initial focus of building a community-facing group was all-consuming, and I did not have the bandwidth to focus on creating a business group as well.

Yet I came to see how independent restaurant owners regularly work twelve- to sixteen-hour days and are constantly overwhelmed by small business ownership. They deal with unpleasant surprises: a broken air-conditioning unit or refrigerator, an angry customer, staffing shortages, or an employee missing a shift. The list goes on and on. Giving them more information to act on or work with is just not enough or helpful. They do not have enough hours in the day to be able to use and benefit from this information.

To help them, we needed to take another step into their world and actually execute on ideas and deliver money or tangible benefits for their business. I decided very early that Takeout 25 would focus exclusively on activities that would actually increase revenue, reduce cost, foster collaboration, or build community. But seeing how Jimmy built camaraderie among his fellow restaurant owners, and beginning to understand how overwhelmed the average restaurant owner was, further inspired me to create a Takeout 25 restaurant owners/managers group. It was a simple Facebook Messenger chat group with a handful of local owners I had come to know over the first few months of Takeout 25.

Overcoming Initial Challenges

I assumed that as business owners they would have many common challenges and triumphs to share and discuss. However, the first few weeks of the group was dead silence, with an occasional awkward message from me trying to get a conversation going. I quickly realized that the trust required for open dialogue on shared interests just did not exist. Everyone was so focused on their own business and were white-knuckling through the stress and uncertainty brought on by the pandemic. They considered each other as potential competition, as they were all vying for a slice of the same pie. A few weeks in, I knew that if I were to build trust and break the silence, it was important to prove that together we could make the pie big enough for everyone to have a bigger slice. With the Takeout 25 community group continuing to grow, the owners quickly realized that more of the local disposable income was coming their way. The pie was indeed growing, and their own slice was safe and in fact expanding.

This prompted a few owners to chime in with an occasional question, which were met with some tentative guarded responses from others in the group. It was still not the open dialogue and collaboration that I had hoped for. I stuck with the process of adding new owners to the group one at a time and betting that sooner or later the conversations would take off.

Over the next few months, there was a slow but steady increase in restaurant owner engagement. I could see them starting to share a laugh and slowly getting a feel for each other. Just like in any group, there were folks who engaged more and there were others who would silently listen. The breadth of topics discussed also expanded over time. If someone had a slow day or week, they would check in with the group. If someone needed extra freezer space, they would ask the group. If someone needed a service provider, they would reach out and ask for recommendations. In each instance, the quantity and quality of the advice received improved over time. Being a small business owner can be a lonely and scary place. They quickly realized that this need not be. They were all in the same boat trying to navigate the same rough sea. They just needed to figure out how to row together.

Takeout 25 also benefited restaurant owners in surprising ways, some of which I was not aware of until I read this story from Tom, a longtime resident of Oak Park. This prompted more owners to want to come be a part of Takeout 25 and the Takeout 25 Owners/Managers Group.

Uniting the Business Community

Takeout 25 Oak Park is one of those rare ideas that everyone embraced. The idea of helping our local restaurants by spending $25 a week provided a much-needed lifeline during the COVID pandemic, especially for our smaller and often immigrant-owned restaurants. As someone who knows a restaurant owner, I can say she was grateful for the increased exposure for a different reason. Like many small businesses, she was not very tech savvy. A third-party had set up a website using her business name, and another created a Facebook page with her business name. Through Takeout 25, she was able to redirect online traffic to her restaurant while she dealt with the tech issues, which took months to resolve. Since then, I've noticed that other small family-owned spots also didn't have a digital presence and benefited greatly from customers helping direct the community to their restaurants.
—**TOM GULL**, Oak Park resident

The Takeout 25 Restaurant Owners/Managers Group started in March 2021, and it was July before occasional meaningful conversations started to happen. Based on what I had seen so far, I was convinced of the value these conversations had for the restaurants. To make it more consistent, the only option was to get the owners together physically. I realized that while I had met several owners as I brought them to the group, many had never met each other. Many knew each other by name and over social media, but I felt they could all benefit from sharing a physical space, getting to know each other, and unwinding over some drinks and food. So the first thing I decided to do as the pandemic receded a bit was to organize a Takeout 25 Owners/Managers Meetup.

The First In-Person Takeout 25 Owners/Managers Meetup

The first Takeout 25 Owners/Managers Meetup happened in April 2022 at a local restaurant, Taco Mucho. It was organized after Takeout 25 was set up as a not-for-profit. The mission of the not-for-profit and the setup of the Takeout 25 board are covered in part 2 of this book but are mentioned here in our description of the meetup.

Taco Mucho had a space that was perfect to host thirty to forty people. We were not sure how the turnout would be, but we spent considerable time planning for the event. I presented the event concept and draft agenda to the Takeout 25 board. We then refined it further to arrive at the final agenda. The event had two segments. We would welcome the owners with some drinks and have them assemble in the side room. This room was set up with a projector and whiteboard stickies for the wall. It was set up to run a workshop.

The first segment would be business focused. We would start with a quick presentation of the Takeout 25 journey, its mission as a not-for-profit and how it planned to serve the group in the future. Once the forty or so participants were on the same page, we set up a group activity. We split the group into three teams. Each team was given a topic for discussion, and the discussion was facilitated by a Takeout 25 board member. The three topics were increasing revenue (topline), reducing cost (bottom line), and fostering collaboration. Over the next thirty minutes, the teams discussed and generated ideas in each of these categories. Then each team identified the top two ideas from the list

Uniting the Business Community

they generated. The team presented their two ideas to the main group, and the six ideas (two each from the three groups) were left up on the wall for group members to vote on. Each group member was given a set of color-coded sticky dots that they could use over the course of the evening to indicate and rank their support for an idea or ideas. At the end of the meetup, the ideas were ranked based on the votes received, and the top vote getters were prioritized for execution.

It was a fun and meaningful exercise that the group enjoyed being a part of. The joint physical activity and having to move around the room together to read and discuss acted as an icebreaker. It was also an effective use of the group's time together to understand shared priorities.

The second segment was focused on socialization and networking. Taco Mucho served up some delicious food and cocktails. This was the perfect setting for the group to get to know each other as people. The pandemic had been stressful for everyone in the room, and the opportunity to unwind a bit with others who shared the stresses of the past two years was a relief for everyone in the group. A great time was had sharing stories, jokes, laughs, drinks, and food. Overall, a very pleasant and productive event.

This whole experience solidified my belief that in-person get togethers would need to happen periodically, and we decided to organize these meetups every six months (April and October). Each meetup has been fun and productive to keep the group aligned on its key priorities and ensure progress on each of these priorities.

Early Collaborative Initiatives

My aspiration for how this owners group could help every participant was tested when Delia's Kitchen, a local breakfast joint, was completely destroyed in a fire on November 23, 2021. The fire left the owner, Veronica, and her staff completely stranded. I reached out to Veronica, and she was in shock. She was talking to her insurance people and evaluating her options, but her main concern was her staff and their livelihood. I collected details about her staff and shared that with the Takeout 25 Restaurant Owners/Managers Group. Within hours, most of Veronica's staff found new jobs, and within a couple of days, everyone was back to work. This made me realize the power of the group as a support mechanism for local restaurants.

RAVI'S FACEBOOK POST

NOVEMBER 23, 2021

Dear Takeout 25 family,

The fire at Delia's today is shocking and tragic. Just when you think it cannot get any tougher for these small local businesses, it does. I'm encouraged by the outpouring of support that I have witnessed on social media in the last few hours. However, I think a coordinated response would be beneficial for the businesses affected, especially because we don't have a full assessment of the damages yet. I'm writing to say that I'm in touch with Veronica (owner of Delia's) and hope to better understand what would be helpful for her and her staff over the next day. We can then coordinate a response that

Uniting the Business Community

> really helps her business and staff along with other affected businesses.
>
> I know that there are several GoFundMe pages created and several ideas generated. This is great. If we can help link all of these efforts to this thread, then it would be beneficial to figure out a path forward and tap into appropriate resources. I would really appreciate that.
>
> PS: I want the businesses to know that we have their back. And I'm forever thankful to be part of such a caring and giving community.
>
> #takeout25

Today, it warms my heart to see the conversations between restaurant owners on the Facebook Messenger group. Owners root for each other's success and share tips and resources with each other. If a restaurant has a broken HVAC system or needs freezer space to store some extra meat for a party order, fellow restaurant owners are there to help. Owners share their frustrations over a slow business weekend or compare notes on the business prospects over a holiday. It also became a forum for restaurants to collaborate on important social issues like the Black Lives Matter movement and the response to the war in Ukraine.

When a local brewery closed in the fall of 2021, the handmade Black Lives Matter banner that hung in the brewery's window needed a new home. The owner and the group that created the banner reached out to me for help to find the banner a new local home. I shared this in the Takeout 25 Restaurant

Owners/Managers Group. Within minutes of me posting, Jimmy Chen from Poke Burrito claimed it. It's now proudly displayed in his shop window.

I am one of the people who created the "Black Lives Matter" crocheted banner that is currently hanging in Poke Burrito. We connected with Jimmy through the Takeout 25 Facebook group after Oak Park Brewery closed and our banner lost its home. I was so grateful our piece found a place in our community and with a restaurant owner that was so clearly dedicated to the community.
—**THERESALYNN O'CONNOR**, Oak Park resident

When war broke out in Ukraine, a local restaurant owner who grew up in Ukraine and has family and friends there wanted to help the situation on the ground. In addition to creating bagels in Ukrainian colors of yellow and blue to raise funds, he made solidarity banners for display on storefronts. He asked me if other owners would be interested in displaying these banners at their restaurants. I posted in the Takeout 25 Owners/Managers Group, and twenty-five restaurants expressed their willingness to display the solidarity banner.

Small business ownership can be a very lonely place, and the Takeout 25 Owners/Managers Group has made it a little less so for the owners and managers in our network. Our owners understand and appreciate the fact that they have each other's backs and the community collectively has their backs.

Uniting the Business Community

This is a personal story about the power of connection during the pandemic.

In the early 1990s when AIDS was raging, for many with AIDS, isolation from the larger community—the result of judgment, fear, and anxiety—was an all-too-familiar problem. I worked in the field then and was sometimes the only person in touch, and touching, people who were shunned and apart. The quote from E. M. Forster appeared on a poster from the AIDS Pastoral Care Network, and it became my mantra—only connect. In the ensuing years, all my work has been to foster connection. Words and actions coming together to generate love. It is enough. And it is sometimes a hard thing to do.

> Only connect! That was the whole of her sermon. Only connect the prose and the passion, and both will be exalted, and human love will be seen at its height. Live in fragments no longer.
> —E. M. FORSTER, Howards End

Fast forward to March 2020, when the COVID-19 lockdown broke connections on a much wider scale. In my little pie shop at the corner of Harvey and Harrison, the crew (we employ people with and without disabilities) were sent home. But who knew pie was essential? We never really closed, because a small group of dedicated people, despite our own anxieties about the virus, continued to make pie. Pie connected us to the community. The streets were deserted. Shopping—standing in lines to get into places, moving through shops following arrows up and down aisles—all became our routine. Out of our isolation, we cobbled together our new lives, all the while seeking the connection of words and passion that grow love. The phone was a lifeline for many customers, long chats came with orders, and we listened to everyone.

Then, along comes Ravi Parakkat and Takeout 25. Organized to promote connections between people and food, to give people a forum to talk about what they found delicious all over our community, it daringly promised to keep us in business, and it turned out to offer so much more.

Early on, I met with Ravi, and we talked about my dream of connecting with other restaurant owners. You see, from the beginning I was always very isolated in my little shop. When you are a small business owner, and you are intimately part of the day-to-day work, lack of time means there is no way to step out of your place, meet others, and share the joys and burdens of doing what you love! Ravi believed it could happen through Takeout 25. Of course! He began what is now an amazing network of restaurant owners and managers.

Let me tell you a little about what this network gave to its members. When COVID meant supply-chain delays, a member would ask how to get... say, a certain cup. Someone might offer an extra case they had available. Another would share where they had found them. They might also consider a sustainable option—typically more available. We would all be enriched by the conversation. When repairs were needed, recommendations would come. It was a marketplace of ideas. What was most evident was the innate generosity of people who feed others because it brings them joy. This sharing continues to this day.

Eventually we shared things like "Having a tough week. Anyone else?" The flood of caring responses was so helpful! It broke the isolation we would have felt so deeply without this network.

Uniting the Business Community

In response to the pandemic, we created a new way to be connected—many, like me, for the first time. When the pandemic eased and we were able to meet together in person, it was wonderful to put faces to the names. We already knew each other and celebrated a kind of homecoming.

The simple power of "only connect" cannot be underestimated. In ordinary and extraordinary ways, Takeout 25 enabled connections that were life-giving in the midst of the great sorrow surrounding many lives.
—**MICHELLE MASCARO**, owner, Happy Apple Pie Shop

Today we have almost one hundred restaurant owners/managers in the Facebook Messenger group. This was built one restaurant at a time. I have met and explained the Takeout 25 concept and its evolution to each owner/manager and then added the ones who were keen to be a part of the group. We have made this Messenger-based communication model work, but it is not ideal for a many-to-many communication model. A Facebook Messenger with a hundred participants can be quite unwieldy. Conversation threads get buried quickly and are difficult to search. Because it is free and requires no additional investment from anyone involved, however, we continue to use it. We have a Takeout 25 Restaurant Owners/Managers Facebook page as well. We use the page and the Messenger chat in conjunction to manage our communication flow. In the longer term, it would be nice to have a communication tool that fits our needs as a group.

KEY TAKEAWAYS

- Being a small business owner can be a lonely and scary place.
- Working together has benefits collectively and individually.
- Building trust is important for collaboration, and it takes time and facilitation.
- People are inherently good. We just need to show them that they can protect their interests and meet their obligations without letting go of the good in them.
- Virtual interactions have become the norm, but periodic in-person interactions are important to deepen virtual relationships and build trust.

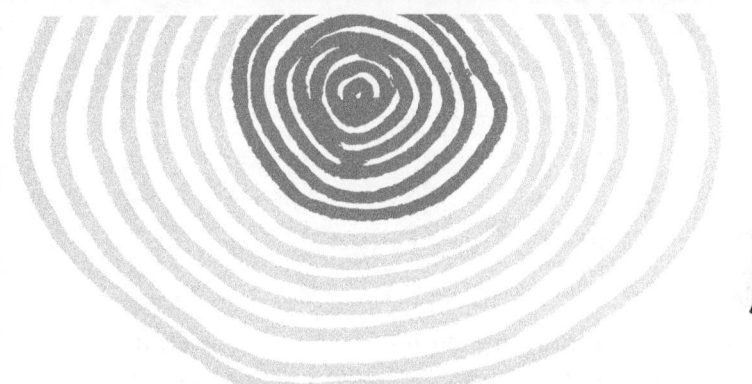

5

Group Administration and Its Moderation

I love being part of Takeout 25! Even beyond helping boost local restaurants, Takeout 25 has been a way for the community to connect in a positive, uplifting manner!

—CARLY WILLIAMSON

WITHIN WEEKS, THE Takeout 25 community grew to twenty-five hundred, then five thousand, then to ten thousand by late 2021, each with stories to tell and photos to share. People wrote about enjoying old favorites. They learned about new places and shared their experiences of eating new food. And we learned about one another. People cared. And exuded positivity.

That simple rule—be positive—resonated and reverberated throughout the community. Instead of finding fault with a restaurant, the Takeout 25 community preached love for new restaurants and old favorites. Community members like Mary Bunn, Beth Harvey, Sarah Manongdo-Joya, and several others became regular, trusted contributors, telling of their potsticker/pad thai/pasta fagioli eating adventures.

—**JOHN HARRIS**, principal at a5 Inc. and Takeout 25 board member

Upholding the Positivity Rule

While I had social media accounts since 2007, I used them only to stay connected with and informed about my globally distributed family. I started my campaign to get elected to the Oak Park Village Board in the middle of the pandemic. This forced me to more actively participate and listen to local social media groups and channels. This was the primary channel to meet community members and understand community concerns better.

The conversations I witnessed on social media in 2020 were toxic. People were tearing each other down without hesitation. I was also beginning to realize that these conversations were unproductive. This was killing the sense of community as opposed to building it. That is not what I wanted for Oak Park, and that is not what I wanted to see reflected in the Takeout 25 community that I hoped to build. I wanted to build a community and a positive experience for everyone who participated in it. This prompted me to view Takeout 25 as a social experiment. The fundamental question for this experiment was, Can a positive space be created and maintained on social media? What would it take to do this?

My hypothesis for the experiment was that the physical separation from the person you are interacting with on social media made it easy to be negative and offensive. Typically, we respond to what we see on social media with a reaction (like, dislike, love, angry face, sad face, etc.) or a comment. With a reaction or comment, the bar for appropriateness and decency seems to be significantly lowered when the person you are reacting to is not physically in front of you. Add a few drinks and the frustrations of a global pandemic, you have the perfect concoction for disastrous online behavior. Conversations quickly spiral out of control and never in a good way. I realized that setting an explicit positivity rule as an entry and participation criteria for the group was the only viable way to set community expectations for engagement. I was also worried that negative comments about a restaurant experience could sink the very restaurants we were trying to save. We did not want to be another Yelp! So we added the positivity rule from day one.

> **RAVI'S FACEBOOK POST**
> NOVEMBER 20, 2020
>
> Welcome to this group. Thank you for joining. Please invite your Oak Park friends and spread the word. We need our entire community to come together quickly here to help save our local restaurants and keep our restaurant workers employed.
>   Do remember to stay positive with your comments. There will be some negative experiences but please refrain from sharing them in this group. Our words here could be the difference between sinking or saving our restaurants.
> #saveourrestaurants
> #carryouttocarryon
> #takeout25oakpark

People have occasionally referred to Takeout 25's focus on positivity as "toxic positivity." I've been asked whether the positivity rule curtails freedom of speech. It does not, and it's not even a situation where freedom of speech applies. However, I do believe that very often people use "freedom of speech" as an excuse to be mean to people they do not like. I also believe that freedom of speech, civility, and positivity can all coexist.

I was not prepared for what followed. There were plenty of people who, upon joining the community, quickly forgot about the positivity rule. The rest of social media had conditioned their behaviors. We had to constantly moderate and facilitate hard to keep conversations on track and positive. Yelp had also conditioned people's behaviors to be able to go write a negative comment about a restaurant and for those reviews to hurt the restaurant. The Takeout 25 philosophy was to encourage members to take their negative experiences and provide constructive feedback directly to restaurant owners. Takeout 25 was happy to facilitate conversations with and convey feedback to restaurants on behalf of customers.

RAVI'S FACEBOOK POST

DECEMBER 12, 2020

Dear Takeout 25 family,

 Sharing my post from Nov 20 below. With us growing so quickly, I wanted to reiterate the importance of staying positive with your comments. Please share your constructive feedback about any negative experiences either directly with the restaurant, or PM me and I'm happy to share that with the local restaurant. Please refrain from posting it on this group.

> We do not want our comments here to amplify negativity and sink a restaurant instead of helping them survive.
>
> Our words matter. We all make mistakes so please forgive and forget.
>
> #saveourrestaurants
> #takeout25oakpark
> #carryouttocarryon

The Role of Moderators

We started Takeout 25 as a Facebook group because of how popular Facebook was in Oak Park among thirty- to seventy-year-olds. During the pandemic, this was the most effective way to reach and communicate with a broad group of community members who shared our commitment to community and had the economic means to support our mission. We set it up as a public Facebook group to make it easier for more people to join the group. We wanted to keep the barriers to participation as low as feasible.

While the rules of positivity and the focus on promoting local brick-and-mortar food businesses was nonnegotiable, we set the group to automatically approve all member posts to reduce barriers. This worked well. People were posting about their local food experiences. The photos and the descriptions shared in the group were inspiring others in the community to dine and support our local restaurants. This fueled the early growth of the group, with each day seeing hundreds of members sign up to participate.

As the group grew into thousands of members, this model was tested. Strong moderation became important to ensure the group stayed positive and its focus on supporting local food businesses was maintained. The early volunteers who were part of the Takeout 25 launch in November 2020 doubled up as administrators and moderators for the group, and we all learned the art of moderating a Facebook group as we went along—from each other and from our own mistakes.

Over 70% of the Takeout 25 community are women. The Takeout 25 community has adults of all ages and reflects the racial diversity of our communities. We have always tried to build the moderator group in the image of the community we serve. We've typically had six to eight moderators, with two or three men and five or six women. We've also made an effort to bring in representation from all the Takeout 25 communities. However, the most important criteria is their demonstrated commitment to our community and our mission.

While the posts were preapproved when we started the group, as soon as we realized the group was getting too big for preapproval to work, we decided to change the groups setting to make approval required for all posts. This decision turned out to be an important one. Once the post made it into the group, it was much harder to control. Actions like deleting a post or specific comments, regardless of the reasons or our reasoning, always left folks unhappy and bitter. This was true even when our actions were prompted by offensive comments or posts. That feeling was often not limited to the specific commenter or the poster but extended to others involved in that thread. By participating in a conversation thread, people feel a sense of agency and ownership. Deleting a post or a comment violated that, and it was very hard to provide satisfactory rationale for a moderator's action.

Group Administration and Its Moderation

However, we learned a lot from that experience. We learned about the community, human psychology, and the art of social media moderation.

Very early on, we set up a Facebook Messenger group for moderators of the group. This Facebook Messenger group became the coordination mechanism for us to share our learning and discuss approaches to specific posts and comments. Our decision to make approval required for all posts was a life- and time-saver. Previously, we had to be plugged into every conversation in the group, ready to respond/moderate in real time. This got stressful at times, and we had to monitor the group continuously. Once we made approval required, this stress was reduced. We could discuss the implications of posts and determine their appropriateness for the group before deciding to approve or reject. We could also warn each other of potentially problematic posts before they got approved so we could monitor the comments and avoid them getting out of hand. This gave the moderators some breathing space.

The positivity rule on Takeout 25 came as a huge relief for many in our community. Many had given up on social media because of how negative and toxic it had become. Several reached out to thank us for creating a space that was positive and a group that fostered a sense of community. Once everyone realized we were serious about the positivity rule, community members started reporting negative posts and comments. This self-policing aspect of moderation was unexpected but eased the administrative burden on the moderators. This was when I finally realized the social experiment of creating a positive space on social media can work. My confidence that we could bring people together to build and transform society grew with the size of Takeout 25 and the engagement of its members.

Our growth and success created a different challenge. Requests to post and promote to the group increased exponentially. Nonfood businesses, GoFundMe pages, and air duct cleaners all wanted a piece of the action. Some of these were easily rejected but some were trickier. The moderators weighed in on the merits of each potentially controversial post and the majority vote/voice carried the day. While most people understood our reasoning for rejecting their post, some had a hard time accepting a rejection. This strained relationships, especially for me as the visible face of the organization in our community. In hindsight, the decision to remain focused was key to our success, and I'm glad we stuck with it.

In addition to the type of businesses we plan to support as a group (i.e., local, independently owned, licensed, brick-and-mortar food establishments), we had to define what we meant by "local." As I mentioned in chapter 3, we expanded from being focused on just Oak Park to include Oak Park's immediate neighbors. The geographic focus did not come easy and was a cause for much angst in the Takeout 25 group. Expanding past Oak Park kicked off a debate, and then with every expansion, there would be some concerns raised in the group or directly with me. It's fascinating how we make the community we live in a part of our identity and reject the notion of inclusion of others who live just a stone's throw away.

A big part of effective moderation is for the moderators to clearly understand the mission of the group and the implications of a misaligned post making it into the group. There is a place for clear rules, but there is also room for ambiguity where the moderators have to use their own judgment. We've addressed the ambiguity through a democratic process of moderators sharing their perspectives and aligning on an approach for a post or a conversation thread. Most of these decisions can be handled by the moderators using their own judgment or with group input. Infrequently, there are posts/situations that are particularly challenging, and the group remains undecided even after discussion. In this scenario, there must be a clear leader who can step in and make the call and explain the rationale behind the call.

Regardless of how the decision is made, it's critical that the decision is fair, rule based, and mission centered.

The intention behind the positivity rule was not to always sing the praises of restaurants regardless of their quality of food and service. The goal was to shift the scale of feedback from say, -5 to +5 to a 0 to 10 scale. So rather than use a negative comment/rating to share a suboptimal experience, the group's silence spoke volumes about the quality of a place or lack thereof. The problem with a negative comment is that it never stays objective for long. It just provides others with the opportunity to pile on, and before you know it, the whole conversation is hijacked.

We survived the first month with some bruises and a lot of learning about triggers and topics that risk negative reactions. The pandemic had people on edge, and even benign topics could at times create flare-ups and result in negativity.

THE TAKEOUT 25 EFFECT

> **RAVI'S FACEBOOK POST**
> DECEMBER 29, 2020
>
> This is in response to a post on the group's policy on violating health orders. Please feel free to PM me if you have questions or need clarification on my response below.
>
> Once I post this, I will remove the original post/thread.
>
> This group was formed with a focus on takeout as an option to balance between restaurant survival and community health during these difficult times. It was not created as a forum to denounce a particular restaurant's actions. It was designed for the community to come together to let our local restaurants know that we have their backs and with the firm belief that together we can get through this. And this group has done just that, and I thank you for that.
> #saveourrestaurants
>
> Having said that, I've personally had conversations with restaurants on this topic, stressing the importance of adherence to state and local rules and will continue to do so. I encourage folks to have direct conversations with restaurants and provide feedback OR PM me if you would like me to share the feedback. You can also share concerns with the local or county health department for further investigation, if you believe it's warranted. Please do not use this forum to share and amplify your negative feedback or denounce a restaurant's actions.
> #takeout25oakpark
>
> Hope this clarifies. Please PM me for further clarifications.

With preapproval turned on, when negative posts or potentially problematic posts came up for approval, moderators could engage the poster to better word the post, and if that did not work, reject the post. The comments could not be controlled or set for approval, but by this stage, the community was starting to self-police by reporting any negative comments in the group to the moderators for review and removal. It's not perfect, but this model has served us well since.

KEY TAKEAWAYS

- Positivity has to be encouraged and can be engineered.
- Be clear on your mission and focus on it to the exclusion of distracting priorities.
- You will make people unhappy. You have to be okay with this.
- Policing the social media community by community members (distributed policing) is far more effective than centralized policing. Enforcement, however, is more consistent and effective when centralized.
- People will make mistakes. The focus must be to acknowledge the mistakes (publicly, if required), learn from them (use them as examples to teach), and recover from mistakes (build on trust and credibility).
- It's more important to be fair than right. Being fair always pays off in the long run.

6

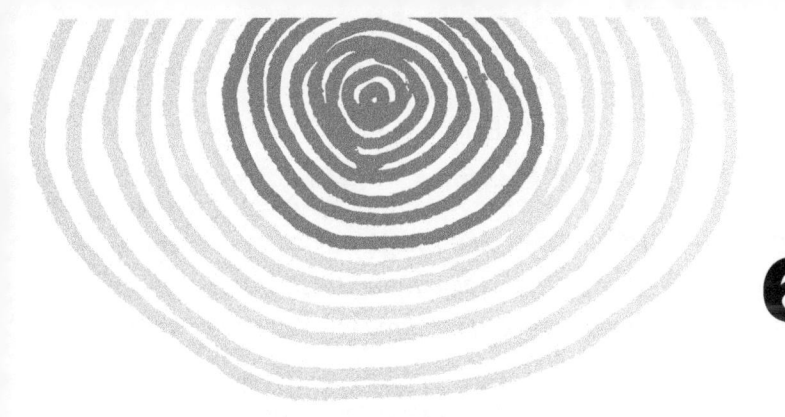

The Significance of Early Events

New Moms is so grateful for the support we've received from Takeout 25 through their Taste the Town events. Takeout 25's mission is not only to highlight local restaurants and small businesses but also to introduce patrons to a diverse and delicious array of cuisines they might not have encountered otherwise. To have this initiative step up during the pandemic to make these important community connections was inspiring to see and be a part of. Takeout 25's dedication to community building is what every community needs. They found a creative (and in this case, tasty!) way to bring people together, support local small businesses, and ensure the critical work that New Moms and other organizations do within our community continues. Thank you for your partnership in championing the dreams and potential of young moms. Together, we are making a tangible difference in the lives of families, one meal at a time. Thank you, Takeout 25!

—NEW MOMS

IN NOVEMBER 2020, I read an article in the Wednesday Journal that challenged local residents to spend $25 a week to keep the lights on for local restaurants. This challenge resonated deeply with me—it felt both achievable and impactful, and I knew I could play a part in making a difference. I joined the Facebook group mentioned in the article, enjoying the food pictures and restaurant experiences posted by other members of the community, and made my own list of restaurants to try.

As my list of must-visit restaurants grew longer, I began to envision a grander endeavor. Instead of visiting each eatery one by one, I wanted to embark on a gastronomic adventure and try them all at once! This ambition led me to reach out to Ravi with a bold proposition: the creation of the ultimate takeout experience. With the generous donation of a fellow resident's stimulus check, we secured the initial seed funding needed to kickstart our ambitious project. Thus, Taste the Town was born, not merely as a culinary extravaganza but as a charity event to support Housing Forward and bring awareness to our vibrant food scene. Through a Facebook group dedicated to local restaurateurs, we identified six restaurants and three dessert venues to participate in Taste the Town. We were determined to elevate our local restaurants, not burden them, and priced the entrée and dessert bags appropriately so that each restaurant received full payment for their meal contributions. The remainder of the ticket price went to Housing Forward. In our first year, we sold 262 of 300 tickets. Drawing on my extensive background in project management and nonprofit experience, we were able to leverage our partnership with Housing Forward to incorporate technology tailored for nonprofits. The 1.5 months we spent coordinating logistics prior to the Taste the Town pickup date were crucial for establishing processes that could be replicated in the future. The Nineteenth Century Club generously provided us with use of their event space along with their walk-in cooler.

The Significance of Early Events

To ensure a smooth flow, we staggered pickup times, limiting meal retrievals to one hundred per hour. Restaurants delivered meals, volunteers assembled the bags, and orders were placed in participant vehicles—all under the watchful eye of the health department during the challenging pandemic lockdown. The buzz that had originally started when Taste the Town was announced on the Takeout 25 Facebook page increased to a steady hum as restaurant owners enthusiastically engaged with the community.

The collaborative spirit of these eateries rallying together in support of Housing Forward, a cherished local Oak Park nonprofit, increased the anticipation and excitement. This collective enthusiasm reached its zenith on our February delivery day as community members eagerly waited in their cars (or chatting outside of their cars!) for their food pickups. Even though the traffic was backed up to Lake Street, no one minded, because finally, after months spent apart, we were together (somewhat) supporting our neighbors in need.

The long-term impact of Takeout 25 and Taste the Town extends beyond mere culinary delight; it's about building connections and fostering a sense of community. We've seen this community spirit strengthen among the restaurants within Oak Park and across the boundaries of our village, uniting the people of Oak Park with its surrounding towns and neighborhoods.
—**ALLISON CUMMINS,** Takeout 25 moderator

Takeout 25 grew its membership by more than one thousand people each week in December 2020. The holiday season and the restrictions the pandemic placed on activities like traveling and visiting friends and family helped Takeout 25 grow. People looked at virtual ways to meet and engage with local friends, family, and community members. Takeout 25 created the perfect opportunity for community members to engage and get excited about food.

Why We Organized Events

As we approached 2021, I was very concerned about the core winter months of January through March that were right around the corner. These months are traditionally the slowest business months for restaurants. This reality, coupled with the unknown impact of the pandemic, was a scary proposition for local restaurant owners. I was concerned that once we left the holiday season behind and entered the new year, community engagement would be harder than it was during the holiday season. This got me thinking of fresh ideas to engage the community, and events were the logical option. Over the holidays, we planned a few small events for the new year and announced these plans to the community with this post.

RAVI'S FACEBOOK POST

DECEMBER 31, 2021

Dear Takeout 25 family,

  The last 6 weeks have been a rollercoaster ride. Our family has grown to 6,000 members. Together, we've inspired communities across the nation to join this movement to help save local restaurants. However 1 in 6 restaurants in the US have already closed due to the pandemic and—every year—January through March are the leanest months for restaurants.

The Significance of Early Events

Together, we have made a tangible difference already, but our toughest months are ahead of us.

The discussion on community health and safety was an important one—one that needed to be had transparently, acknowledging all perspectives before deciding on a solution.

Now the time for discussion and debate is over, and we have a path forward.

As we close the curtains on 2020 and start the new year, let's renew our focus on our core mission: community coming together over takeout food to help save our restaurants. I re-emphasize the importance of staying positive in this group, and I am personally committed to creating a positive space on social media: something we all crave during these difficult times.

Let's also have some fun together! As we start 2021, we have exciting events planned for the group. All events are centered on takeout food and furthering our core mission. This includes photo contests, watch parties, virtual shows, etc. (Watch this space for detailed announcements on events!). In the meantime, sit back and enjoy great takeout food with your family and share your pictures here.

I truly believe that together we can make a difference in people's lives. Our local restaurant owners and staff are also our neighbors and friends. Let's make a difference in their lives. Let's make a difference!

On behalf of the Takeout 25 core team, Happy New Year!
#saveourrestaurants
#takeout25oakpark
#carryouttocarryon

Brainstorming and Execution of Event Ideas

Here are some of the first event ideas and how we carried them out.

Gift card giveaway – OPRF Chamber – For two months, The Oak Park-River Forest (OPRF) Chamber of Commerce partnered with Takeout 25 to give away $50 worth of local restaurant gift cards every week to Takeout 25 Facebook group members. Group members who received the most likes on their Takeout 25 Facebook posts about local takeout experiences won the gift cards.

While this idea drove some engagement, it was clear that more ideas were required.

Community Trivia – Madison Street Theater (MST) – Takeout 25 members registered online for the free Quizlet trivia game played virtually over Zoom. The concept was simple. Community members would order takeout food and enjoy it with their family while playing a game of trivia virtually with the rest of the community. It was fun for the community and also a huge success thanks to folks like John Paulett, who helped host the virtual event on a remote technology platform.

RAVI'S FACEBOOK POST

JANUARY 5, 2021

Dear Takeout 25 family,

 Madison Street Theater and Takeout 25 are sponsoring an exciting community event on Sunday, January 17: MST Family Trivia Night. Here is the plan. Order takeout for the online event starting at 6:00 p.m. on the 17th and join

The Significance of Early Events

> Madison Street Theater for a free trivia game. Get the whole family together to enjoy local restaurant food while we play a community-wide trivia game. Save the date/time now (Jan 17, Sunday, 6:00 p.m.) and watch this space for event access information.
>
> If you are a local restaurant owner and would like to participate as an emcee or with a promotional mention (no charge to you), please let us know in the comments and we will reach out to you.
>
> No one is making money on this except, with your support, our local restaurants! So Takeout some food and Come Join Us at MST Family Trivia Night. Our goal is to build community, so please share with friends and family. Madison Street Theater and Takeout 25 are proud to be part of such a great local community.
>
> #saveourrestaurants
>
> #takeout25oakpark

Community Dinner – Taste the Town – In January 2021, as we were planning the gift card and the trivia events, I received a message from Carrie Banks, who worked with Housing Forward, a local not-for-profit addressing homelessness. She had an idea for a fundraising event for Housing Forward in partnership with Takeout 25. I was interested but just did not have the time or bandwidth to pursue the idea.

A day or so later, I received a message from Allison Cummins (another Oak Park resident) who expressed how much she enjoyed being a part of Takeout 25. In her hometown, she was involved in a successful event that brought restaurants together for a ticketed event with the proceeds shared between the participating restaurants. She was reaching out to share that event experience and to explore opportunities to get more involved with Takeout 25's work. She wanted to volunteer her project management skills to the cause.

A day later, Kelly Moran Cuneen reached out to me with an offer to donate $500 from the pandemic stimulus check her family received to initiatives to support restaurants while also feeding the hungry. I saw the synergies between these three reach outs and brought Carrie, Allison, and Kelly together. These three independent messages and discussions that followed coalesced into what has since become Takeout 25's signature event: Takeout 25 –Taste the Town.

The original iteration of Taste the Town was a virtual ticketed event. We brought a set of restaurants and dessert places together to create food and dessert packets for a fixed-price ticket. The ticket proceeds were equally divided between the participating restaurants. A portion of the proceeds would go to a beneficiary nonprofit. In the first instance, that nonprofit was Housing Forward, since this event was a direct result of Carrie's reaching out.

We believe that impactful local nonprofits represent the values of a community. The relevance and importance of having a local nonprofit beneficiary for the Taste the Town event was that, in addition to supporting local restaurants, we wanted to build a community consistent with our shared values. We used our partnership with nonprofits to promote our community's social values.

The Significance of Early Events

This event was significantly bigger and more complex than the events we organized previously. To bring such an event together with zero capital, we needed to figure out a few things:

- **Identifying and recruiting restaurants.** We needed a set of eight to ten restaurants. This was well before we started the Takeout 25 Restaurant Owners group. At the time, I knew a few owners but not many. I started reaching out to owners and quickly realized we would be able to get a good lineup of restaurants serving diverse food and dessert options.

- **Ticketing platform.** Allison recommended a not-for-profit platform called Run Signup/Give Signup that she had used in the past. The fee structure was steep, but the company was itself a not-for-profit technology company exclusively serving the event ticketing needs for not-for-profit events. It was also easy to get it up and running quickly.

- **Clear understanding of local health protocols and permitting requirements.** Each restaurant needed a temporary permit to provide food for the event. As the food was prepackaged for takeout, the restaurants had to cook and cool the food to be able to safely serve it to the community.

- **Venue to pack the food and pick it up.** We needed a centrally located venue that was convenient for community members to drive by and pick up the food. The venue needed space to receive/store the food while maintaining the temperature prescribed by the health department. It also needed space to assemble the food bundles for pickup. The Nineteenth Century Charitable Association in Oak Park was the perfect venue that

THE TAKEOUT 25 EFFECT

met all the criteria and, most important, offered the space to us for free.

- **Packaging and instructions.** The restaurants created printed heating instructions for us to include, and we bought branded tote bags to package the food for customers.

Finally, we needed enough community members to support the event by buying tickets. And, boy, they did.

Taste the Town Savoring Success
Food-focused Fundraiser Raises $38K and Organizers Hope to Repeat Event
by **Melissa Elsmo**, March 2, 2021

<small>This article was originally published in *Wednesday Journal* and appears here with permission.</small>

Take Out 25 Oak Park, the online community dedicated to supporting local restaurants and bakeries through the COVID-19 pandemic by placing copious carry out orders, hosted Taste the Town on Feb. 23. The inaugural event raised $38,000 for Housing Forward and nine Oak Park restaurants and bakeries.

"I am so thrilled to share the financial impact of the Taste the Town event," said Ravi Parakkat, Take Out 25 creator and a current candidate for Oak Park village trustee. "We blew away all our goals."

Funds raised through ticket sales were dispersed through a predetermined formula. Housing Forward earned $9,323 by taking a portion of each bag sold as well as additional donations. Billy Bricks, Kettlestrings Tavern, Mora Asian Kitchen, Poke Burrito, Tre Sorelle, and Wild

The Significance of Early Events

Onion Tied House provided a range of food options and each restaurant received $3,917. A dessert bag featuring an array of sweets from Kalamata Kitchen, the Happy Apple, and Sugar Fixe Patisserie, earned each establishment $1,682.

"Every dollar from the event has gone toward helping our local restaurants survive and feeding people experiencing homelessness," said Parakkat.

Taste the Town, organized by Allison Cummins and executed by Take Out 25 volunteers, drew a crowd of hundreds to The Nineteenth Century Club on a chilly Tuesday evening. Lines of cars snaked in both directions on Forest Avenue awaiting the socially distant, drive-thru style delivery of their "ultimate take-out bag."

Jimmy Chen, owner of Poke Burrito, and his wife worked shoulder-to-shoulder with volunteers to get things done in time to meet the segmented pick-up schedule demands. In fact, most participating restaurants including Tre Sorelle and Mora Asian Kitchen left staff behind to help fill take-out bags with petite pulled pork sliders, diminutive apple pies, lasagna Bolognese, curry chicken and pastel-hued macarons.

"Even though we were in cars it felt good to be part of a crowd when we picked up the food," said Paul Clark, longtime Oak Park resident and Taste the Town participant. "Oak Park has a long history with these types of social events. This type of event defines a community and the fact it was done well makes people want to do more of the same thing and encourage others to participate in the future."

Cummins said she felt nervous leading up to the event but left thrilled by the success of the evening and inspired by the overwhelming positivity exhibited by people picking up their Taste the Town bags.

"I feel like the pandemic has made people feel a little helpless," said Cummins. "Taste the Town was a tangible way people could make a difference at a time they were looking for a way to help."

Parakkat and his team acknowledge there were a few hiccups at the first-time event and apologize for any errors they made along the way. While the team is aware there is room for improvement, they have already identified small switches to enhance the experience and are excited at the prospect of repeating the event soon with Housing Forward or another not-for-profit organization.

"We would love to do this event again in April or early May," said Cummins. "Restaurant owners really took a chance on this event, but they seemed happy with how it turned out. I want to thank the restaurant owners, everyone at The Nineteenth Century Club, and the entire Take Out 25 community. We could not have done this without everyone working together in this collaborative environment."

"Taste the Town came together really well," said Parakkat. "The food was top notch, and this event reinforces my choice to make Oak Park Home."

Oak Park's Taste the Town Event is now being replicated in Madison, Wisconsin.

It was wonderful to see the community come together and breathe a collective sigh of relief in the middle of the pandemic. It was then I realized that collectively we could get through this.

The Significance of Early Events

While the pandemic was still active, we organized two more Taste the Towns, each time supporting a different nonprofit beneficiary: the Day Nursery (early childhood education) and New Moms (helping young mothers find their footing). We experimented with the space and refrigeration needs by renting a mobile refrigeration van and also used the beneficiary nonprofits' space and volunteer base to help execute the events. Being a virtual group without a formal structure came with immense flexibility but also restricted our ability to independently execute events and initiatives.

During this phase, we leveraged our nonprofit partners to receive and distribute funds. We were not a legal entity and did not have a bank account at the time. We set up our ticketing platform for our events so the event proceeds would go to our partner not-for-profit's bank account. As a political candidate running for local office, I was also not comfortable receiving and distributing payments from the general public. I wanted to avoid any perception of financial inappropriateness. This was best managed by ensuring the funds involved were transparently handled through established and reputable nonprofits we were partnering with.

Operationally, not everything went perfectly at these early events. We had close calls, with some restaurants struggling to get the event permitting process figured out. At the first event, we underestimated the number of volunteers required to package the food we received from the restaurants for customer pickup. We also had a restaurant fail the health inspection, resulting in us having to discard their entire batch of food (we still paid the restaurant in full). On one occasion, a participating restaurant had a smaller portion size that did not match a resident's expectation. He walked up to me to inform me that this was not India or China where we could get away with smaller portion sizes. I apologized profusely but also reminded him of our mission (the reason why we were all doing this in the first place). It was a reminder that providing value for money is important even when you are doing it for a good cause. People are motivated by what's in it for them while seeking broader community impact. I was also reminded that racism and prejudice are alive and well!

Whenever we faced a challenging situation, help came from completely unexpected sources to support our events. We are grateful for all the support, and without that ground-up support, we would not have been able to organize these events successfully.

Today, Takeout 25 Taste the Town is an annual in-person event where we bring the community together in June to celebrate all things local. We've expanded the concept of tasting to include more than just local food to tourism, entertainment, art, and everything else unique about the community. Taste the Town has helped us raise well over $100,000 to support local restaurants and causes. Most important, we've had fun doing it.

The Significance of Early Events

KEY TAKEAWAYS

- Expand the cause by encouraging event ideas from members.
- Allow members to contribute their money and talents to help the cause.
- The answer to these two questions must be an emphatic *yes* for events you decide to execute:
    - Is it simple to execute?
    - Have you maximized the number of people and organizations that will benefit from this event?
- Make sure what you raise through an event will cover the event costs at the very least.
- Make sure everyone associated with the event (residents, sponsors, partners, etc.) find value in their involvement.

7

Navigating Politics

Takeout 25 was (and remains) a beacon of light for the entire community. For many of us, food is closely intertwined with community and belonging. Takeout 25 was a way for us to create a community around food even in isolation and give a boost to our amazing local restaurants.

—TANYA ROBIN FISHER

I DON'T WANT TO USE hyperbole and say that Takeout 25 was unique, but it's a bit amazing and also heartening to see this movement grow from an idea nurtured by a few people, with a simple management and few rules, into a model of something that not only sustained/saved many small businesses but also helped connect village and area residents in a way that they didn't connect before.

It wasn't a government program, and it didn't arise out of an already existing local nonprofit (both types of organizations played important roles in other parts of pandemic mitigation). It arose out of the unique circumstance of small businesses unable to do as much business as before (because indoor dining was banned) and people stuck at home because of workplace and school closings (and tired of banana bread and with a little extra money to spend *because they weren't commuting to work and spending lunch and dinner money out of the community).*

With a narrow goal, some dedicated volunteers, and skillful use of Facebook for word-of-mouth advertising, Takeout 25 could move from ideation to new money flowing to local businesses in a matter of days/weeks. Takeout 25 became a model of how a community could step up and step in when the government and banks dragged their feet in helping local businesses.
—**PAUL CLARK**, Oak Park resident

Takeout 25 started in Oak Park, Illinois, a community known for its liberal values and left-of-center politics. It's also an educated, engaged, and opinionated community with a median annual household income of $93,000. The pandemic-induced isolation saw community members take to social media to air their views. I was shocked by how brutal community members were to each other. It was like people wanted to be right, and even more important, they wanted to prove the other person wrong. Winning petty arguments on social media seemed to matter for many.

Political Context: National to Local

In the US, divisions made apparent by Donald Trump's presidency were in the midst of a political transition to Joe Biden's presidency. The pandemic heightened the divisions between political parties, and individual states and municipalities pursued divergent approaches to this major public health event. Election results, mask mandates, and the amount of pandemic stimulus were all part of the national debate, with red and blue states expressing positions and policies along party lines. This fueled the social media discussion about the right and wrong ways to act.

This was true even in a community like Oak Park. While there were fact-based discussion groups on Facebook giving residents locally relevant data and facts, like the Oak Park Coronavirus Group, these discussions often devolved into preferences based on political identities.

This environment posed a challenge for Takeout 25 because we wanted to remain politically neutral with positivity as one of our core values. It was also challenging to build community by bringing people together in this polarized environment.

The Interplay of Personal Politics and Takeout 25

In 2021, COVID-19 restrictions continued to place a heavy burden on Oak Park restaurants. For many, temporary closures became permanent as they could no longer have customers come inside and enjoy a meal. Restaurants that survived the initial onslaught of forced closures faced new hurdles as rules around distancing, masking, and proof of vaccination were put in place. For many, the key to success centered on the ability to pivot long-term from an in-person model to carryout and delivery orders. This was our most pressing business issue in the 2021 local municipal elections that Ravi and I were both a part of. With state and federal aid still on the horizon, providing relief for Oak Park eateries was paramount to candidates seeking a position on our city council (village board).

Takeout 25 provided a lifeline by encouraging Oak Park residents to spend $25 per week on takeout orders from local restaurants.

THE TAKEOUT 25 EFFECT

This model accomplished several things: it highlighted the need for takeout orders to become a bigger revenue stream; it provided a dollar threshold that fit the price point for many Oak Park restaurants; and it created a space for the community to rally around local restaurants, which were as diverse as its residents. As a not-for-profit, it provided all of these things with no additional cost burden to businesses already financially overwhelmed. Takeout 25 became the ultimate "give back" program benefiting businesses that fed our families, helped us celebrate life events, provided jobs for local residents, and supported our local economy.
—**LUCIA ROBINSON**, Oak Park village trustee

The fact that I was a candidate for local political office during the first six months of Takeout 25's existence added another layer of complexity for the group. It was a struggle to keep the group politics-free. It was an even bigger struggle to keep my political detractors from politicizing my every action and decision on Takeout 25. I had to be extremely disciplined with my actions and communications.

As a relative unknown in my community with no prior political experience, my chances of success in the local municipal elections were slim. Takeout 25, through its success, had given me positive name recognition in the community. It had associated me with getting things done for the community even before I was elected. It strengthened my case as a candidate and contributed to my eventual victory in the consolidated municipal election on April 6, 2021. What surprised me about my election was my margin of victory. I was the highest vote getter in a field of six. Takeout 25 was one of the primary reasons for these results.

However, the road to that outcome was fraught with tension and drama. My political detractors would use the Takeout 25 forum to air their political displeasure with my candidacy. My every action and post were judged. I was clear from the beginning that politics has no place on Takeout 25. I personally was committed to not using the Takeout 25 forum to promote my political platform, and I wanted others to do the same. This was easier said than done.

A couple of experiences I had during my political campaign best describe the impact of my politics on Takeout 25 and vice versa.

Right after Christmas Day in 2020, the level of activity in the Facebook group spiked. One of the posts was about a local restaurant owned by our town's then mayor, Anan Abu Taleb. Someone had taken a picture of the new heated outdoor patio they had installed. This prompted comments about the health and safety implications of such a space during the pandemic. The moderators' approach was to direct the concerns to the qualified local health department to inspect and determine safety and compliance rather than speculate based on a photo on social media. This prompted negative comments about the mayor that were irrelevant to the conversation and inconsistent with our mission. We asked folks to refrain from making negative remarks or politicizing the conversation. This only fueled the fire and prompted further attacks.

Finally, I stepped in, deleted comments, and ultimately kicked some people out of the group. This prompted the dispelled members to go back to their respective corners on social media and bad-mouth me. These attacks were not based on facts. It was a testing period in Takeout 25's evolution, and I got to understand my community and some community members better. It was important that Takeout 25 remained fair to all restaurants in the community despite the pressure. Takeout 25 emerged stronger from that episode as a lot of people joined because of the controversy and a lot more people joined and stayed because we had maintained the positivity rule in the face of significant pushback.

A few weeks later, the owner of a local restaurant, a Black woman, decided to endorse my political candidacy. Her endorsement was based on the beneficial impact Takeout 25 had on her business. She was experiencing an over 30% increase in sales revenue attributable to the Takeout 25 effect. My election campaign was racially charged with me competing with a slate of Black candidates campaigning for Black representation on the village board. So the endorsement of a nonBlack candidate by a local female Black small business owner did not sit well with some of the supporters of the Black candidates in the race. These supporters threatened the poor small business owner with a boycott of her restaurant as retribution for endorsing my candidacy.

This experience was a wakeup call for me. I had not expected local politics to get this ugly. I was committed that my politics should not adversely impact the very restaurants and restaurant owners that I worked so hard to support with Takeout 25. I reached out and asked this business owner to take down her endorsement post from social media. I had recorded an endorsement video featuring an interview with this restaurant owner that never got used in my campaign.

The criticisms from my political detractors have evolved with Takeout 25. They started with criticizing the idea, but when the idea quickly became a movement, this criticism died down. As Takeout 25 grew to thousands of members, detractors questioned my ability to manage and moderate a large group on Facebook. It was quickly replaced with criticism of the positivity rule and my strict moderation of the group to enforce it. With time, this criticism also became irrelevant as more people joined the group as a direct result of the positive space that we were able to create through Takeout 25.

While similar flare-ups occurred consistently during my election campaign, they have occurred less frequently since my election in April 2021. Once Takeout 25 became a not-for-profit, the criticisms shifted to the financial management of the group and the inappropriateness of a local elected official managing a very influential local group (their words, not mine). I finally realized that regardless of what I do, there are going to be people who do not like what I am doing and how I am doing it. I used every criticism as an opportunity to reflect, learn, and adapt my approach. Beyond that, I prioritized transparency in my actions and decisions. I focused on the mission and the impact on people's lives and refused to get bogged down by unsubstantiated criticism.

Vaccine Politics and the End of the Pandemic

Takeout 25 was formed in response to the pandemic. Our strategies and tactics were designed to counter the roller-coaster ride of uncertainty and anxiety resulting from the pandemic. We wanted to save local restaurants by bringing the community together in their support. It was a delicate balance and needed constant reminders to help the Takeout 25 group understand and adhere to it.

By spring 2021, there was cautious optimism that an mRNA vaccine would be available soon. By the summer of that year, the timing and efficacy of these vaccines were the topics of passionate debate. At the same time, waves of COVID-19—and in some cases, new strains of the coronavirus—were emerging, with every part of the world experiencing the pandemic a little differently and countering their realities with unique policies and approaches. While there was significant confusion and thousands of people were still dying daily, the collective consensus was that the end was near.

This did not stop people from fighting over the most effective approaches to see the pandemic through. Mask mandates were politicized in the US, and the impact of remote schooling on the learning gap was becoming apparent. The pandemic had forced the entire world to pause and rethink every aspect of life and indeed life itself. People reached different conclusions about what they wanted from life, and many doubled down in its pursuit. The stimulus checks provided the household savings required to make new and different choices about the future as the world emerged from the pandemic.

The stimulus checks were an effective and important strategy to counter the early impact of the pandemic, but final batches of stimulus created extra liquidity and resulted in inflation. This had a significant impact on many businesses, especially the food business. People's changing work preferences resulted in worker shortages. This, combined with the inflation pressures, increased the cost of serving food at restaurants. These inflationary pressures were exacerbated by global and local supply chain bottlenecks.

Navigating Politics

Together, this squeezed restaurants on the supply and cost sides of the business. The inability of small restaurants to pass on these costs to their customers while the pandemic was still around left restaurant owners in a very vulnerable position. The transition out of the pandemic started to feel like jumping from the frying pan into the fire itself.

The vaccine story took several twists over the coming months. Moderna, Pfizer, and Johnson & Johnson came out with their vaccines. The discussions about their relative efficacy quickly turned to how best to prioritize vaccination for the population. Moderna and Pfizer ended up being the popular options. The old and vulnerable were prioritized for the early doses. Vaccination status and entry for restaurant patrons based on vaccination status then became a flash point. In addition to vaccine deniers, the politicization of vaccination—just like masking before this—presented challenges. In the US, these debates became proxies for political ideologies, and it further divided an already polarized society.

KEY TAKEAWAYS

- People will criticize your actions and decisions. Use this criticism to challenge your thinking and approach. Learn and adapt, but don't get bogged down by them.
- Focus on acting in ways that are consistent with your values and convictions.
- DO NOT spend your time and talent to prove other people wrong; instead, focus on proving yourself right.

"Food as a Social Lubricant"
Supporting Local Restaurants; Empowering Communities

Rachel Kathleen Hindery, June 15, 2021

This article was originally published at AxiomNews.com and appears here with permission.

When indoor dining temporarily ended in Oak Park last fall during the Chicago, Illinois suburb's second wave of COVID-19, some residents took to social media to share their opinions on the balance between public health and small business survival.

"There was a lot of debate but no real solution," Oak Park Trustee Ravi Parakkat said of the controversy. Instead of taking a side, Ravi said he did some math. He realized that if 10,000 people spent $25 dollars per week at local restaurants, it would generate $1 million per month; about $10,000 per month for each of Oak Park's approximately 100 restaurants.

"That $10,000, in my mind, represented additional revenue that would help them survive the pandemic—cover basic costs like rentals or leases and some payroll," Ravi said.

Just over two weeks later, after Ravi talked to stakeholders and residents, Takeout 25 officially launched with a website, Facebook page and local media coverage.

About six months later, Takeout 25's Facebook page has more than 8,000 members. Other communities bordering Oak Park have joined in.

Similar initiatives have also started in communities across the Chicago Metropolitan Area and in other American states including New York, Ohio, Indiana, Texas and California.

"The focus is in the simplicity of the math," Ravi said. "Every community should go through that and see what is really required" based on their population and number of restaurants.

Giving people a specific dollar amount to spend each week gave them something tangible they could do, instead of a broader campaign to shop nearby, Ravi said.

"Letting people know they are actually having an impact on the local economy and they are part of a broader movement and they are contributing to a cause is important," he said. Through participating with other nearby communities, Takeout 25 widened its support. "Both in terms of the restaurant business and local businesses and in terms of the community we're not that far apart," Ravi said.

"We have to cross those borders; we have to build bridges, but the way to do that are ideas like Takeout 25," Ravi said. "We are spending zero taxpayer dollars. There should be no reason to resist that."

People experience the excitement of sharing a favourite meal or restaurant, while getting to know the people behind their favourite places.

"Businesses cannot join as businesses," Ravi said of the Facebook page. "They have to join as the owners and the managers and the staff; as people."

Social media exposure helps restaurants with marketing, even if they don't have a marketing team. "It enhances some of those capabilities, but it also takes people from having nothing to having something," Ravi said, describing it as "systemic help" for the restaurant industry.

When Ravi launched the Facebook page, there was only one rule—no negativity. "Once you go through that initial hump of reconditioning people and giving them a new frame to interact, they turn around and it becomes a self-monitoring engine," he said.

"I consider food as a social lubricant," Ravi said. "It definitely brings people together. If you're looking to build a diverse community, the food in that community has to reflect that diversity."

Experiences around food, Ravi said, are some of the "micro moments" that empower community, or even attract new residents.

With between $3 and $4 million generated in additional revenue, Takeout 25 is poised to outlast the pandemic. Ravi envisions turning it into a nonprofit.

"While it started with the frame being 'survive,' as we come out of the pandemic, I'm looking at 'how to help the local economy thrive' and how do you use technology to enable that in a not-for-profit model which is aligned with the community?'" he asked.

Ravi added that he is actively working to make this a reality.

Through Takeout 25, people are connecting their dollars to their values; whatever they're able to contribute. They're also ensuring there will be places to gather and connect.

"It helps us time travel to a different point in our life," Ravi said. "We've made friends at specific restaurants. We've gone and celebrated moments in our lives. We've created memories that are important to us—and that is what a community is ultimately about."

PART 2

Harnessing a Movement

Takeout 25 is a complete paradigm shift on how we think about the business in our community and the impact an individual citizen can have. The pandemic has been a bleak time for small business, and Takeout 25 put the power in the people's hands to make a difference . . . It's very powerful.

—SEAN HENNESSY
President of Delivery First
and Takeout 25 board member

8

Founding the Not-for-Profit

This group is very active and really helped bring together several communities, both consumers and business owners. We share information and all the latest updates on this page. It's a very engaged group that will go on regardless of the pandemic.

—ALICE VANKO

IT HAS BEEN SO WONDERFUL to see the journey of Takeout 25 from its earliest days of formation into a well-branded, multi-community organization that it is today empowering neighbors to support local food businesses while working to eliminate food insecurity.

When Ravi sought help establishing Takeout 25 as a legal entity, I introduced him to my husband, Steve Wiser, who directs the business law clinic at DePaul University, which provides emerging small businesses with legal guidance. That was a springboard for creating Takeout 25 as a not-for-profit organization.

My day job is CEO of Housing Forward, an early nonprofit partner benefiting from Takeout 25's mission. As a service and housing provider for our neighbors experiencing homelessness, *restaurant meals became a critical part of feeding our clients during the pandemic. Hundreds of clients were in our care, and providing three meals a day was becoming a real challenge. We were reliant on volunteers and caterers, and it just made such good sense to engage area restaurants.*

The Oak Park Homeless Coalition and Ravi's restaurant network organized, coordinated, and delivered hundreds of weekly meals to feed our shelter and interim housing clients. Our staff and clients were SO grateful to have a consistent variety of delicious meals. It really made our work easier while mutually beneficial to our local small businesses.

The unwavering support of Ravi and Takeout 25 is proof that a community that gives is a community that thrives.
—**LYNDA SCHUELER**, CEO, Housing Forward

Evolving Past the Pandemic

Takeout 25 was very successful in its original mission, and it had created a grassroots movement to support local restaurants. This movement ensured that many local businesses and livelihoods were saved. The concept had spread to other communities in a very short period, but would the concept be relevant once the pandemic receded? Should we kill the group or sustain it after the pandemic? How would the group stay relevant?

These were the questions I was grappling with in May 2021. It was very clear to me that keeping the group alive beyond the pandemic had to be based on the group's continued relevance to the community. To establish this, I decided to talk to restaurant owners and community members about the future. I was overwhelmed by the positive support and requests to keep the group going. The pandemic had forced changes in the food business model. Some of these changes were here to stay, but others, like indoor dining, were reverting to the pre-pandemic normal. However, the community and the business community realized the power of collective effort. It was also clear that while the COVID-19 pandemic might be receding, the next crisis could be right around the corner. Once I knew there was support to move forward, I had to decide what shape the entity would take. The conversations quickly turned to shaping the future.

I started Takeout 25 to support the community through a difficult time, and I wanted Takeout 25 to remain a gift to the community as we moved forward and have a life beyond me. With this in mind, I read about potential future models and spoke to several people in my network to understand how best to achieve the outcome I was hoping for. The consensus and the conclusion I reached was to set up Takeout 25 as a not-for-profit. In part 2 of this book, I'll talk about the experience of setting up and running a not-for-profit to harness the Takeout 25 movement to deliver value for the community.

Back to the Drawing Board

Once I had decided that setting up Takeout 25 as a not-for-profit was the best course of action, it was time to execute. I did not take this on lightly, and I had no prior experience doing something like this. So much had to be thought through, discussed, and decided to set up an organization. The fact that it was going to be a not-for-profit increased the compliance and procedural formalities. My ignorance about the process of setting up a not-for-profit was my single biggest advantage. If I had realized how long and laborious the process would be, I would have had second thoughts. I started down this path in May 2021.

Naming the Initiative

My starting point for this journey was to revisit the name. Takeout 25 was a great name that represented our focus during the pandemic, but did it make sense for our ongoing efforts? After a few conversations and much thinking, I concluded that there was value in retaining the name. We could build on the local brand awareness and goodwill. We had the opportunity to creatively use the name to mean "Taking out 25," and this could expand our focus beyond just takeout food without changing the name. With this decision, I set out to articulate the vision, mission, and values for the not-for-profit.

Defining the Vision, Mission, and Core Values

Food was central to the Takeout 25 mission. We believe that food represents the taste and diversity of a community, and we believe in a model that focuses on enabling local independently owned food businesses to make a more livable and desirable community. Takeout 25's tagline is a result of this vision:

"Building thriving and sustainable communities"

The fact that we kept the tagline plural ("communities" instead of "community") was intentional. We knew that if we successfully created a model to address our scope and aspirations, then replicating that concept across communities would be a real possibility. The reason I'm writing this book is to document the Takeout 25 story and explore the possibility of replication to other communities.

Our vision and mission build on this belief and add more specificity to our scope and our long-term aspirations.

Mission: Takeout 25 will empower local small business economy while addressing food insecurity and enabling sustainability.

The three mission elements:

- Empowering local food businesses economically
- Addressing food insecurity
- Enabling sustainability

Economic empowerment of restaurants was the reason Takeout 25 was created, and that continues to be a priority. Our experience working with restaurants through the pandemic exposed us to local food waste issues and unaddressed food needs in the community. It made us aware of the scourge of plastic packaging in the food industry and the sustainable practices that restaurants and the community at large could benefit from. Many in our community (a fairly affluent one) were going to bed hungry. This was a bigger problem in the Austin neighborhood just east of Oak Park that was also part of Takeout 25's service territory. We were also seeing strong signals that the pandemic had increased the socioeconomic disparities in our society. Locally, we saw an uptick in demand at our food pantry and an increase in homelessness. The pandemic had also exposed the vulnerabilities in the food supply chain and offered opportunities to make it more sustainable.

The three areas of local economic empowerment, food security, and sustainability were not just relevant today but topics that would be relevant and more complex to solve in the long-term. The scale of these challenges and their long-term relevance to community building contributed to their inclusion in our vision and mission.

Core Values: We wanted the vision and mission to focus on "why" and "what" and not get bogged down on "how." We coupled the vision and mission with our core values:

- Positivity
- Community focus
- Sustainability
- Impact
- Innovation

The vision and mission, along with our values, provided a basis for decision-making. It provided the clarity we sought to make strategic and operational decisions, but more important, it helped us stay focused by eliminating options that were not aligned.

I did not have a time dimension to our mission, partly because I did not want to set the organization up for failure as we had a 100% volunteer-driven model and partly because life was already too rushed and I did not want to chase artificial timelines. In my experience, this could lead to confusion and unnecessary stress. I would rather focus on impact and grab the right opportunities, aligned with our mission and values, as they came along. Often, these opportunities have a natural timeline that would guide our actions. This was a departure from everything I had learned and experienced on the topic in B-school and my business career since, but it made sense for me when it came to Takeout 25.

Crafting the Emblem: Logo Design

Now it was time to design a logo that represented the vision, mission, and values of Takeout 25. A conversation with Allison Cummins, who had helped organize Takeout 25 Taste the Town events and was now a Takeout 25 group moderator, made me aware of a platform called Designhill that I could use to crowdsource designs. The platform did this by creating a contest for designers globally, for a small fee. I checked out the platform and was intrigued by the possibilities. It was cost-effective and easy to use. The contest prize money of $250 was to be deposited with the platform at sign-up as a precondition for using the platform. We had to upload a design brief to help contestants create logo designs consistent with the brand. In a day or so, designs started flowing in, and in a few days, we had over two hundred submissions from a global pool of designers.

Some of the designs were easy to eliminate, but once I got it down to the initial top fifteen, further eliminations became really difficult. I relied on the Takeout 25 moderator group to get the number down to five. I then worked with the top five designers to refine their designs. I engaged the Takeout 25 family for the final selection. I wanted the community to feel a sense of connection with the brand. So I packaged up the three designs that were in the final shortlist and posted the contest in the Takeout 25 group. The group overwhelmingly favored what is now the Takeout 25 logo.

THE TAKEOUT 25 EFFECT

This logo, a tree with dining utensils in black for its trunk and green leaves with the name Takeout 25 in bold letters along the base of the tree, was designed by an Indonesian designer, Mubarak Designs. The Takeout 25 community made the perfect choice. The designer shared how he had conceived the logo and the significance of the different elements in the design and how they represented the brand. I shared this perspective with the Takeout 25 community in my post below.

RAVI'S FACEBOOK POST

AUGUST 13, 2021

Dear Takeout 25 family,

We have our final logo! I wanted to share some details I received from the designer about himself/herself and how he/she came up with this design. He/She is spot on. Great job!

In the designer's words:

"I live in Indonesia. I am 25 years old now, I was born in a poor family and then studied design by myself, with great hope that I can change my family's life."

1. Fork and knife: is a distinctive symbol that is easy to understand for restaurants and food.
2. Tree: symbolizes growth and innovation.
3. Green color: has the meaning of fertility/sustainability.
4. Black color: represents strength and commitment.

So this logo represents solutions for developing the local economy through food supported by a strong community.

Founding the Not-for-Profit

> PS: For obvious reasons, the Designhill platform does not allow direct interactions with the designer outside the platform. So I could not get more information from the designer, but his/her design shop is Mubarak Designs.
> #takeout25
> #saveourrestaurants
> #food
> #sustainability
> #community

Check out the logo at www.takeout25.org.

The other aspect of the logo that is worth highlighting is the word Takeout 25. The "25" is carved out of the letter *O* in Takeout. This takes the simple brand Takeout 25 and adds some depth to it. Highlighting "25" this way can then be applied in the context of all the mission elements of Takeout 25 (e.g., reducing food waste and carbon emissions by 25%).

The Incorporation Process and Board Selection

Now that we had defined the scope, values, and brand for Takeout 25 the not-for-profit, it was time to formalize the legal entity that would be the vehicle to pursue this scope. It was time to find some legal help and to identify a board, which was a requirement to form a not-for-profit.

I reached out to several local contacts for recommendations for a lawyer who could help me with setting up a not-for-profit. One of those I reached out to was Lynda Schueler, the executive director at Housing Forward (the nonprofit focused on addressing homelessness). Lynda referred me to her husband, Steven Wiser, a law professor at DePaul University. At our introductory call, I outlined my plans for this new not-for-profit to Steven. Steven then suggested I work with Abigail Ingram as the legal counsel for Takeout 25, with him playing an advisory role. Abigail, at the time, was heading the Women's Business Incubator at DePaul University and was a practicing attorney. This started two important relationships that were instrumental in the setup of Takeout 25 NFP.

Abigail, Steven, and I got together to discuss the various legal aspects to be considered in the setup of a not-for-profit. In addition to the incorporation of the entity through the Illinois Secretary of State, we discussed its registration with the Illinois Attorney General's office and the IRS tax exemption category it would be eligible for. The IRS has several not-for-profit classifications; based on the nature of activities envisioned in scope for Takeout 25, we decided Takeout 25 should apply for 501(c)(6). This allowed us to operate like a member-based trade association (e.g., chamber of commerce). As an entity that supports local for-profit small businesses (restaurants), this was the only categorization we would qualify for. However, there were elements of our mission (i.e., food security and sustainability) that were social causes that could fit within the 501(c)(3) tax-exempt status. (This is what most nonprofits are classified as.) The key advantage of a 501(c)(3) is that donations and contributions received are tax-exempt for the donor, while for a 501(c)(6) they are not.

Founding the Not-for-Profit

To support the incorporation, Takeout 25 needed a board of at least three members. I wanted individuals committed to our community and the Takeout 25 mission to join me on the board. I spoke to Michelle Vanderlaan and Melissa Elsmo, two people who were familiar with Takeout 25's evolution right from its launch in 2020. Michelle is a local small business owner with sound marketing instincts and an excellent feel for the local small business environment. Melissa was the food editor for the local newspaper who had chronicled the evolution of Takeout 25 to that point. They both said yes to becoming founding board members of Takeout 25 NFP. However, Melissa quickly realized the conflicts that might arise from a role on the Takeout 25 board and her role with the local newspaper, and she had to formally resign from the board shortly after Takeout 25's incorporation. I then invited John Harris, who, like Michelle, was an early believer and supporter of Takeout 25 and owned a digital marketing agency. John said yes without hesitation.

> **RAVI'S FACEBOOK POST**
> AUGUST 25, 2021
>
> Dear Takeout 25 family,
>   Meet the Takeout 25 NFP founding board as we signed the articles of incorporation at the Wild Onion Tied House a few weeks back. I'm fortunate to have these two strategic thinkers and local leaders join me on the board. I'm confident we will push each other's thinking and hold each other accountable as we create an impactful not-for-profit that truly serves our

> community. Thank you, Michelle and John.
> Please support our launch on 11 September.
> https://www.givesignup.org/TicketEvent/Takeout25Launch
> #takeout25
> #takeout25board

Abigail and I met at Buzz Cafe, a local breakfast place, to discuss the further details needed for incorporation, and we applied online. We filed the application and paid the fee online with the Illinois Secretary of State, and Takeout 25 NFP was formally incorporated on May 23, 2021, a little over six months after our start as a group in November 2020. One of the decisions that needed to be included in the articles of incorporation was the fiscal year for the entity. After careful thought, we decided that July 1 to June 30 would help us close the books in time for summer and provide the organization with some downtime to recharge for the next fiscal year. We also discussed the bylaws that govern the not-for-profit, and shortly thereafter we had bylaws drafted ready for the board to review and adopt at our first board meeting. The first meeting of the Takeout 25 Board was September 2, 2021, with Michelle, John and me in attendance and Abigail joining as our legal counsel to help us through the procedures and protocols for the meeting. In addition to adopting the articles of incorporation and the bylaws, we elected the officers of the board: Michelle (treasurer), John (secretary), and me (president).

Leading up to the first board meeting, we set up a bank account for Takeout 25 with Byline Bank, a local community bank. This gave us the ability to start collecting funds that would be needed to support the not-for-profit's activities. We also initiated the applications for registering Takeout 25 NFP with the Illinois Attorney General's (AG's) office as a charitable organization. We then filed the application (Form 1024) with the IRS for the 501(c)(6) status. Both applications came back to us with clarifications, and after a few iterations of questions and responses, both got accepted. The Illinois AG's office took four months; the IRS took over nine months. Our first financial year as a not-for-profit started on July 1, 2021; in August 2022, we became a 501(c)(6). The application submissions and the processing of these applications by the respective agencies took up the full financial year and then some.

Over the course of that first year, I invited Rob Guenthner and Sean Hennessey to join Michelle, John, and me on the Takeout 25 board. Rob, a lawyer who served as the chief legal officer for Oak Street Health, was also one of the owners of the Kettlestrings group of restaurants based in Oak Park. Starting with Kettlestrings Tavern just before the pandemic, Rob and his team grew the Kettlestrings brand to include Kettlestrings Grove and Betty's Pizza & Pasta over the course of the pandemic. Sean, on the other hand, was the president of a local food delivery service, Delivery First. He had significant operations experience in the hospitality industry with brands like Aramark. Both Rob and Sean are Oak Park residents and very community-minded. They each brought perspectives that were unique and important to our mission.

Securing Funding and Financial Management

Takeout 25 was started with zero capital investment using freely available resources and services provided by generous volunteers.

THE TAKEOUT 25 EFFECT

We wanted to try to decouple the need for money while seeking to solve some of our most pressing social issues, and it worked. From the very start, all our initiatives and events were designed to be cost neutral. We raised money for our events through sponsorships, ticket sales, and donations. We relied on volunteer labor. We also received internship grants and in-kind services to support our efforts. Before we were set up as a legal entity in Illinois with a bank account at Byline Bank, we always spent everything we raised on our nonprofit partners and participating restaurants. In those early days (the first six months or so starting November 2020), I spent well over forty hours per week on Takeout 25. I invested my personal money to support Takeout 25, but this was manageable thanks to committed and community-minded sponsors like Susie Goldschmidt at Byline Bank, Arthur Paris at Carnival Grocery, Bethany Brown DeCaspers at The Cadence Group, Sean Hennessey at Delivery First, Sean Olis at Guaranteed Rate, Michelle Vanderlaan at Sugarcup Trading, Arthur Hoffman at Tidal Commerce, Chris Griffith at Oak Park Bank, Andrew Palomo at Pillar Financial, Philip Jimenez at West Cook YMCA, and Dorian Gallo at Federated Foodservice, to mention a few.

I'm the market president for Byline Bank in Oak Park-River Forest. I have been a restaurant owner myself, and I was concerned about the effects of the pandemic on local restaurants. As a user of social media, I witnessed Takeout 25's launch on Facebook and its growth and evolution into an impactful not-for-profit. Inspired by how it was bringing the community together to help local restaurants, I started buying hundreds of $25 gift cards ($15,000 worth) on behalf of Byline Bank from local restaurants for Byline customers and as

donations to local not-for-profits. This act inspired by Takeout 25's simple idea grew into a relationship with Takeout 25 that involved Byline Bank sponsoring Takeout 25 events and initiatives these past two years.
—**SUSIE GOLDSCHMIDT,** OPRF market president for Byline Bank

As we were pursuing the setup of a not-for-profit, I wanted the organization to have some financial reserves for stability and to have the freedom to pursue its mission. Being a 501(c)(6), Takeout 25 was tax-exempt. However, unlike a 501(c)(3), the donations made to Takeout 25 NFP were not tax-exempt for the donors. This was a distinct disadvantage for our fundraising efforts, but that is something we would have to deal with as a not-for-profit. This choice raised some alarm bells at the local chamber of commerce. The chamber had seen its membership decline during the pandemic and was worried that Takeout 25's entry as a 501(c)(6) would further erode their base. I had to reassure them that my vision for Takeout 25 was very different from the activities the chamber organized. The situation quickly stabilized with each of us focusing on our respective lanes and activities.

Starting in July 2021, our newly formed not-for-profit started receiving some donations. I met with a few key community leaders who were aware of Takeout 25's impact and had the ability to support its future. I was successful in securing their support. We raised over $30,000 in July 2021, and this gave us a great starting point to pursue our mission. The key contributions came from Stephen Schuler, a prominent local philanthropist and business leader. He and his wife, Mary Jo Schuler, have supported several local causes through their philanthropic efforts.

THE TAKEOUT 25 EFFECT

The only wrinkle in this situation was that while Takeout 25 was incorporated as a charitable organization in Illinois with the Illinois Secretary of State's office, we were still in the process of applying for tax-exemption status [501(c)(6)] with the IRS. I was upfront with Stephen about where we were in the process, and he was extremely generous in his support of our efforts. This support continued in 2022 and in 2023, in spite of these contributions being taxable to the donor. In 2021, a couple of other prominent local business leaders, Bill Planek, owner of Oak Park Apartments, and Mike Fox, owner of the Carleton Hotel, joined Stephen to support Takeout 25 financially. This gave us financial reserves that could be used, if needed. We have not dipped into these reserves to support our efforts over the last two years and in fact have added to these reserves. This gives us the ability to commit dollars to pursue the setup of Illinois's first green dining hub in our community and explore full-time staffing.

Now we had to manage our finances, and for this we acquired some pro bono bookkeeping help from a Chicago-based accounting firm and procured paid licenses for Intuit QuickBooks as our accounting platform. The QuickBooks license came with access for three and the ability to additionally set up accountants. Our accountant helped us set up the Takeout 25 NFP books in QuickBooks. I also needed to get it integrated with the Takeout 25 NFP bank account so that the bank transactions would flow through directly into QuickBooks for bookkeeping and financial accounting.

We also had the Takeout 25 ticketing platform from GiveSignup set up with the Takeout 25 bank account details so funds raised through event ticketing would flow directly into the bank account.

Founding the Not-for-Profit

The last operational element that needed to be set up was the Takeout 25 website. When we first set up the group back in November 2020, we used the takeout25oakpark.com domain name. With the setup of Takeout 25 NFP, we had to revisit and revamp the website. I procured the Takeout25.org domain name, and a5 Inc. helped create the not-for-profit's website.

Much of this work happened privately and alongside the work on and growth of the Takeout 25 Facebook group. However, the setup of the not-for-profit was not yet shared with the community (i.e., my Takeout 25 family). It was now time to make this announcement and launch Takeout 25 NFP with a community event. We chose Barrie Fest as the event to launch Takeout 25 NFP in September 2021.

Introducing Takeout 25 NFP at Barrie Fest

> **RAVI'S FACEBOOK POST**
> AUGUST 15, 2021
>
> Dear Takeout 25 family,
>   Mark your calendars. Sep. 11, 2021.
>   It's official! We are now a not-for-profit, Takeout 25 NFP. This will enable us to focus on sustainability and food waste/insecurity in our community while continuing to enable our local restaurants/economy in innovative ways. Expanded Vision, Mission, and Values below. Thanks for being a huge part of this evolution.
>   We are planning a Takeout 25 NFP launch event on Sep 11 between 12:00 and 5:00 p.m. at Barrie Park (In partnership

> with South East Oak Park Community Organization and Clean up Give Back, with Beyond Hunger as a beneficiary). Please mark your calendars. Details to follow shortly.
>
> Of course, there will be food (an amazing lineup of local restaurants), music, and fun activities for kids. We will do it in a safe and responsible manner that balances our need for in-person social interaction/celebration and community health.
>
> #takeout25
>
> #nonprofitlaunch
>
> Thanks to the SEOPCO board, Beyond Hunger, and the CUGB team for their willingness to partner. Much appreciated.

When we decided to launch Takeout 25 as a not-for-profit, we also needed to figure out a community event for the launch—an event that would reflect the values and mission of our newly formed not-for-profit. Barrie Fest, organized by the South East Oak Park Community Organization (SEOPCO), fit the bill perfectly. SEOPCO is a unique community organization that mobilized community voices in southeast Oak Park around the environmental reclamation efforts in Barrie Park in the early 2000s. Barrie Fest was organized as a celebration of these efforts and the successful reclamation of Barrie Park. In addition to being community focused, these efforts also emphasized local environmental sustainability. This aligned with Takeout 25's mission and values. So we decided to collaborate with SEOPCO to not only launch Takeout 25 NFP at Barrie Fest but also mobilize food vendors for the event.

Founding the Not-for-Profit

I have lived in Oak Park for many years and have enjoyed attending and volunteering for various events throughout our village. I began volunteering for Takeout 25 Oak Park when I heard they were partnering with Barrie Fest. I was excited to help, as I knew this festival was lacking food options (aside from a few food trucks). I have discovered new food establishments (that I typically would not have noticed on my own), lots of fun, and friendship. Ravi and Amy Parakkat brought their vision to this festival, and it continues to grow. Takeout 25 Oak Park has evolved from supporting restaurants during the pandemic to creating Illinois's first green dining hub.
—**JUNE STOUT**, Oak Park resident

Over the years, Barrie Fest has grown from a block party to a community event. The partnership between SEOPCO and Takeout 25 has further established this event as one the entire community looks forward to each year. Barrie Fest is organized the second Saturday in September each year. September is Hunger Action Month. To reflect the food security mission of Takeout 25, we partnered with two not-for-profits, Beyond Hunger and Austin Eats, as beneficiary nonprofits for the last two editions of Barrie Fest. We share a portion of the event proceeds with these not-for-profits to support their efforts to address food insecurity. We also partnered with the local chapter of Clean Up–Give Back to help sustainably manage the waste for the event. Clean Up–Give Back is run by a youth board from the OPRF High School and mentored by Adrienne Eyre, a local sustainability enthusiast.

Takeout 25 has partnered with SEOPCO every year since 2021 to organize Barrie Fest for our community.

THE TAKEOUT 25 EFFECT

Happy Crowd Munches through Barrie Fest, Courtesy of Takeout 25
Restaurant-Boosting Organization Launches Nonprofit Model

by **Melissa Elsmo**, September 14, 2021

This article was originally published in *Wednesday Journal* and appears here with permission.

Barrie Fest bustled with community members looking to support Takeout 25 and seven local restaurants serving up a diverse array of dishes at the Sept. 11 event at the park at Lombard and Garfield. Food vendors included Amerikas, Khyber Pass, Kalamata Kitchen, Mora Asian Kitchen, Billy Bricks Wood Fired Pizza, Carnivore Oak Park, Ben's Bar-Be-Cue, Happy Apple Pie Shop and Cafe Cubano.

Takeout 25 sold more than 350 ticket booklets at $25 each giving attendees the option to select three items each valued at $8 from any of the seven vendors. The remaining dollar in the booklet price was donated to Beyond Hunger. Khyber Pass also donated 20% of its proceeds to Beyond Hunger.

Barrie Fest-goers lined up to make their selections from the food booths and, thanks to strong attendance, both Khyber Pass and Café Cubano ran out of food by the end of the afternoon. The seven vendors collectively earned more than $8,000 at Barrie Fest.

"Barrie Fest and the Takeout 25 launch were absolutely fantastic," said Ravi Parakkat, Takeout 25 founder and now a village trustee. "We had a much larger turnout than we expected, and we would love to partner with SEOPCO again in the future."

Founding the Not-for-Profit

SEOPCO is the South East Oak Park Community Organization. The group began in the early 2000s to respond to the contentious multi-year cleanup of environmental contamination of Barrie Park.

The OPRF chapter of Clean Up Give Back was on hand to ensure the event was clean and green. Thanks to high school age volunteers the festival was free of litter and helped bring attention to Takeout 25's focus on sustainability. In addition to working together at Barrie Fest, Takeout 25 and the cleanup group have collaborated to turn some of the take-out related waste generated in Oak Park during the pandemic into a plastic bench that will be installed at village hall in the coming weeks.

"These young volunteers are doing very important work in the community," said Parakkat. "We are so grateful they helped us handle our waste responsibly."

Both the Barrie Fest celebration and the forthcoming bench are signs that Takeout 25 is becoming a permanent fixture in the Oak Park community and beyond.

Takeout 25 started as an online initiative dedicated to supporting restaurants through the COVID-19 pandemic and marked its transition to an official non-profit organization at Barrie Fest by offering branded T-shirts in exchange for a $25 donation. The effort raised $3,000 and funds will be used to help Takeout 25 cover its not-for-profit start up and infrastructure costs.

While all local restaurants will continue to have universal access to the free marketing engine Takeout 25 has become, the new 501c6 is designed to outlive the pandemic and will rely on a membership model to help support dining establishments and enrich the local economy in a variety of ways.

Parakkat acknowledges the not-for-profit is in its infancy but envisions the Takeout 25 membership cost being $25 per month or $300 per year for participating restaurants. The fees will give members the "right of first refusal" on future Takeout 25 events and access to cross community collaborations designed to strengthen the local economy.

"We are very confident in our ability to provide value to restaurants," said Parakkat. "Everything we are hoping to do will enhance the top-line for member restaurants."

In addition to increasing revenue and lowering costs for restaurants, Parakkat aims to facilitate relationships with local delivery services, introduce collaborative initiatives to aid restaurants in bulk ordering eco-friendly take-out packaging and reduce retail food waste by marketing local food overages in inventive ways.

KEY TAKEAWAYS

- Name and logo are important to create a lasting identity for your organizations. Make sure you spend time on it.
- Make sure you are clear on the "why" and "what" for your organization. Articulate vision and mission to clarify this.
- Use your organization's vision, mission, and values to help decide scope and make key decisions.
- Involve the community in decisions when it makes sense.
- Money is neither necessary nor sufficient to pursue your mission, but it's always good to have some in the bank. You can operate boldly with confidence and independence.

9

Managing a Mission-Aligned Not-for-Profit

> *If you love making a difference, supporting local business, and talking food and restaurants, Takeout 25 does all this and more.*
>
> —KIMBERLY GEORGE

KRIBI COFFEE COMPANY sends a heartfelt thank you to Ravi and Takeout 25's incredible work in our community. Your dedication to empowering local food businesses, prioritizing sustainability, and eliminating food insecurity is truly inspiring. In a world that often seems disconnected, the organization serves as a beacon of unity. By encouraging the community to support local businesses, you remind us of the importance of community and the impact we can have when we come together.

Takeout 25's commitment to sustainability is equally commendable. It's a reminder that we can enjoy delicious meals while also being mindful of the environment. Takeout 25 is more than just an organization; they are a catalyst for change. Your aim to build a thriving and sustainable community is evident, and we are proud to

stand alongside you in this journey toward a brighter future. Thank you for being the change we wish to see in our community.
—JACQUES SHALO, owner, Kribi Coffee

For me, Takeout 25 is like a child. We protect and nurture our children to the best of our abilities. This takes time and attention. Leading up to and since its inception as a Facebook group, I was pouring time and effort into seeing Takeout 25 succeed. Without realizing it, I was spending over forty hours every week, if not more, on various aspects of Takeout 25. I wanted and needed to spend that time to support the initiative. It was also fun and exciting to see the evolution of the initiative and the impact it was having on people's lives. I had support during the early stages from volunteers like Jayson, Melanie, Allison, and of course my wife, Amy, and I'm grateful for that.

With the urgency of the original mission receding as the pandemic ebbed and the setup of a formal not-for-profit coinciding with my new job with Junior Achievement of Chicago, consistent forty-plus-hour hour weeks would no longer be sustainable for me. I needed to figure out a different support model. The Facebook group administration and moderation was supported by volunteers. The setup of the not-for-profit resulted in an independent board. This talented board offered support and advice in managing the newly created entity and its mission. The restaurant owners were also supportive, especially with participation in events and initiatives. However, running an organization is a very involved activity, and when it's a not-for-profit, the compliance requirements add more effort. The need for additional bandwidth to manage the increasing activities of Takeout 25 was becoming increasingly apparent. I wanted to make sure Takeout 25 remained agile and adapted quickly to evolving needs. Prematurely investing in dedicated staff would restrict our ability to be nimble. We had to design and execute a model where the power of the community members remained the driving force.

Internship Opportunities

The need for help and our preference to *not* hire full-time staff prompted me to explore alternate models. John Harris from the Takeout 25 board had introduced me to a contact of his at Dominican University, a local college, and through that connection, I reached out to the placement office to offer internships to undergraduates. Through this program, we recruited Jakub Kaminski, Takeout 25's first intern. For the next two years, Jake would be an integral part of the Takeout 25 team. Jake was involved in setting up the LinkedIn and Instagram pages for Takeout 25. He helped John's team from a5 Inc. with the setup of the takeout25.org website. He worked with me to help set up the QuickBooks accounts for Takeout 25. He was part of all the Takeout 25 events and initiatives. He grew in confidence, and I would like to believe that he learned and grew through his experience with Takeout 25. Jake will always have a special place in Takeout 25's evolution. He and his girlfriend, Valery, are like family to us and would join us at Takeout 25 events.

It was a paid internship funded through the CareerNet grant program that Dominican University had access to. This grant was capped at $2,000 per year per student. Takeout 25 paid $15 an hour for the internship and limited the involvement to 150 hours to manage the spend just above what the CareerNet Grant would cover. It was a win-win for Jake, Dominican University, and Takeout 25.

> **RAVI'S FACEBOOK POST**
> DECEMBER 9, 2021
>
> Dear Takeout 25 family,
>   I would like to introduce you to Jakub (Jake) Kaminski, Takeout 25's first intern. He started with us last month on the Takeout 25 anniversary date (Nov 17) and will be with us on this internship for the next 5 to 6 months. He is a marketing student at Dominican U and will be working on projects that are beneficial for his future and also move Takeout 25's mission forward. I hope this experience sets up a bright future for him.
>   He has already helped set up the Takeout 25 LinkedIn business page. Do check it out.
> https://www.linkedin.com/company/80729190/
> #takeout25
> Now I'll let Jake introduce himself.
>
> ---
>
> My name is Jakub Kaminski, but I typically go by Jake (or Kuba for all my Polish family). I am a 21-year-old marketing and management junior at Dominican University. I was born in Augustów, Poland, a small northeastern farmers town surrounded by lakes that is now a resort town. I moved to the US at about 5 years old. After a bad motorcycle accident that left my dad unable to work for a while, my grandma moved

> to America to send money back to us. In the meantime, she saw how much better life was over there and had asked us to come join her. We did. We had it rough at first, living workless with our uncle in Indianapolis until my dad healed (and even literally on the streets for a while) until my dad secured a job as a carpenter.
>
> We managed to rent a small apartment in Chicago and grew up there until 3rd grade. During this time, I felt like I was still in Poland, as we lived almost exclusively surrounded by other Polish immigrants. When my dad managed to secure a job as a diesel mechanic/tech, we moved to my home in Schiller Park that I live in till this day. We truly managed to live out the American dream, and along the way, I managed to meet so many different people and make so many different memories and experiences.
>
> I matured quite early due to all the moving and a focus on my personal as well as educational life from a young age. But that allowed me to make a strong and diverse friend group, and even meet my current girlfriend of 3 years. Today, I live with my mother, father, grandma, and two brothers (one a year younger than me and another 10 years younger). Pursuing my own goals further and trying to get the most out of our travels to the US, so one day I can repay my parents for what they have done for me and my future.

The experience with Jake prompted me to explore the internship model as we started new initiatives in the future. Especially the launch of Takeout 25 boxed water and the launch of Takeout 25

Green Dining Hub. We brought on Zoharia Drizin for the Takeout 25 Green Dining Hub and John Mastrodonato for the Takeout 25 boxed water initiative. More about them later.

Forming Partnerships

As a grassroots movement, Takeout 25 has always believed in the power of partnerships to deliver community impact. Relationships are a stated Takeout 25 core value. We have lived this belief through every stage in our evolution. We approach every relationship with the intent of deepening its scope into a win-win collaboration. We partnered with local restaurants to unleash their collective strength. We partnered with the local media to help tell our story to the community. We partnered with local not-for-profits to align with the community's social values and to contribute to their fundraising efforts. We partnered with community organizations to reach a diverse audience and build community. We partnered to further our impact. During the early days, we expanded to neighboring communities by leveraging partnerships. All these partnerships continue to exist and evolve.

- African American Business Network of Austin (AABNA)
- Austin Eats
- Beyond Hunger
- Byline Bank
- The Cadence Group
- Carnival Grocery
- Collaboration for Early Childhood

- CUGB (Clean Up – Give Back OPRF Chapter)
- The Day Nursery
- Delivery First
- Dominican University
- Federated Foodservice
- Forest Park Chamber of Commerce and Development
- Housing Forward
- Montrose Wholesale
- New Moms
- Nineteenth Century Charitable Association
- Oak Park Apartments
- Oak Park Bank
- Oak Park Homelessness Coalition
- Oak Park Village Health Department
- Oak Park Regional Housing Center
- Oak Park Residence Corporation
- OPRF Chamber of Commerce
- OPRF History Museum
- Pillar Financial Advisors
- Rush Oak Park Hospital
- SEDAC (Smart Energy Design Assistance Center – Illinois Green Business Program)
- SEOPCO (South East Oak Park Community Organization)

- Seven Generations Ahead
- Sugar Beet Food Co-op
- Tidal Commerce
- Visit Oak Park (all the local tourism and entertainment venues)
- Village of Oak Park, Illinois Emergency Response Team
- WasteNot
- *Wednesday Journal* (Growing Community Media)
- West Cook YMCA
- WGN *Outside the Loop* Radio
- Youth Crossroads

Many others are being formed consistently. Our launch of Illinois's first green dining hub, Takeout 25 Green Dining Hub, is a direct result of our partnership with SEDAC. We have collaborated extensively on this effort, and it would not have happened without that collaboration.

In the early days of the pandemic, my sixteen-year-old daughter asked if she could join me on a community cleanup. Picking up litter was a way to be outside, productive, and socially distant. At the same time, Ravi knew that restaurants were struggling and needed help. I didn't know Ravi, but we both were about to begin a journey that wasn't part of "our plan." The community cleanup evolved into starting the Oak Park and River Forest chapter of Clean Up – Give Back (CUGB), where we defined ourselves as "building community through environmental stewardship." The

Managing a Mission-Aligned Not-for-Profit

local chapter of CUGB is unique because it was teenagers who defined the chapter's mission and filled its board of directors. At the same time, Ravi launched a community group, Takeout 25, to provide immediate help to our local restaurants. Our paths crossed when we both incorporated a sustainability component to our respective organizations.

The partnership was impactful right away. The obvious need was managing waste at Barrie Fest when Takeout 25 launched as a not-for-profit—CUGB diverted more than 50% of the waste from the landfill. But as long as some single-use plastics were still a part of the takeout equation, we wanted to find creative outlets and repurpose the plastics. Ravi had an audience; we had ideas. Takeout 25 community members heard our numerous calls. Collecting single-use plastic bags demonstrates upcycling through the park bench that now resides in our community. Takeout containers were melted into an art installation highlighting sustainability issues at the Chicago Botanic Garden. Bread tags, something that most don't think about, were collected by the restaurant's kitchens and customers to help another nonprofit that sells bread tags, a very clean plastic, to fund wheelchairs for kids in need. While Ravi continues to work on minimizing restaurant waste, we're happy to find outlets for what still exists.

The synergistic partnership with Takeout 25 has benefited both organizations, but even more important, it has benefited the community that both organizations serve.
—**ADRIENNE EYER**, Clean Up – Give Back

Workings of the Takeout 25 Board

The Takeout 25 NFP board meets quarterly in the months of July, October, January, and April. The focus of the board discussion is to help the board understand our operational realities and contribute to the strategic direction. Each board meeting includes the following components:

- Reflect on the events and initiatives since the last board meeting to ensure all the board members are operating with a shared understanding of our current situation.

- Review our financial position against our budget and our compliance status against federal and state annual reporting obligations to the Internal Revenue Service (IRS), Illinois Attorney General's office, and the Illinois Secretary of State.

- Focus on a specific topic that we want the board to discuss and offer perspectives. These discussions inform and guide key decisions of the organization.

- Close the board meetings with a look ahead at the key events and activities and board support required for these. As a board, we meet six hours a year. Individually, each board member spends time, expertise, and/or money to support Takeout 25's mission. Takeout 25 is better for it, and I'm grateful for their involvement.

Moderators Group and Restaurant Owners/Managers Group

We have discussed both these topics in detail in chapters 4 and 5 respectively. They continue to be important constructs that enable our mission. We are fortunate to have such a great group of generous, kindhearted, and community-minded individuals to help align the group's activities with the Takeout 25 mission.

Event Coordination

When Takeout 25 started organizing events in January 2021, I was handling them with whatever help I could get. The early events like the chamber gift card collaboration and Madison Street Theater trivia night were executed without significant event planning and management overhead. I was able to manage these myself or with help from folks like John Paulett, a local retired teacher who had volunteered for my election campaign. Once we decided to move forward with the first Takeout 25 Taste the Town event, there were more cats to herd and more loose ends to tie up. Allison's offer to manage the event was very welcome. After all, she was part of its creation. She helped manage three Taste the Town events in 2021 before she had to take a step back and focus on family and her own business.

With the plan to launch Takeout 25 as a not-for-profit at Barrie Fest in September 2021, I had to take a more active role in planning the launch and executing events. This model worked as we started more events like the holiday gift card bundle (December 2021), employee appreciation (January 2022), emergency shelter (February to April 2022), owners meetup (April 2022), etc. I would involve my wife, Amy, to help with certain aspects of these events, especially the day of the event itself. This was based on a combination of her availability and the needs of the event.

By June 2022, as we were closing the first financial year of Takeout 25 NFP (June 30, 2022), I realized we now had an annual calendar with several standing events that were growing in scale and complexity. It was time to get some dedicated help with event planning and coordination. I talked to the Takeout 25 board, and we decided to seek external help for all our events. We allocated a budget of $25,000 in services fees since events were the biggest enabler of our economic enablement mission. We wrote up an advertisement for the position and placed it on LinkedIn. Days became weeks and weeks a month and we had no takers. This was when Rob, a Takeout 25 board member, casually asked me if my wife, Amy, would be interested in the role.

I had not considered that possibility, but the more I thought about it, the more it made sense. We consulted with Amy, our legal counsel, and the rest of the board and created a process to pursue this without my involvement, considering the obvious conflict of interest. Amy was already doing some of this work, and this gave her an opportunity to formalize that role and create more dedicated space for it in her schedule. This resulted in Amy signing up to be Takeout 25's event coordinator. While she was already helping with some aspects of Takeout 25 events, she started to take a more active role in managing events starting December 2022.

KEY TAKEAWAYS

- This is the opportunity to create efficient decision-making and execution models. Break all conventions.

- The perspectives needed and the constraints involved are specific to an organization or a situation. Get creative with the situation you are in.

- Say yes to partnerships. Yes, all of them.

10

Essential Initiatives and Their Alignment

> *Takeout 25 engaged and mobilized the community to support local businesses. This support saved businesses and saved jobs. Amazing!*
>
> —MICHELLE VANDERLAAN

THE PANDEMIC CHALLENGED the restaurant industry and the people in our communities who owned and worked at restaurants. In parallel, the pandemic also resulted in more families that struggled to put food on the table. When Takeout 25 offered gift card bundles for various restaurants, I thought it was a great opportunity to support our restaurants while also supporting the folks in our communities who were especially challenged during the holidays. I had asked Ravi if there was an option to donate gift cards to folks in our community who had a need, and he agreed to accept the donated gift cards to help address food insecurity in our community. He asked if it was okay to share what I was doing. There are a lot of good, kind people around us, and I believe there is so much willingness to help other *people, but sometimes we just need a spark, a reminder, or a simple idea to generate action. If Ravi was going to share what I had done, I didn't want people to just read it. I wanted to give people encouragement to take action also, so I had told Ravi I would match what the community would come together and donate. We impacted 141 families as a community.*

—MARINA MONDELLO, Oak Park resident

All Takeout 25 initiatives serve one or more of our three mission elements of economic empowerment, food security, and sustainability. Some of these initiatives have become an integral part of our recurring annual calendar, some are one-time efforts, and others are ongoing efforts. They have all helped us innovate and create partnerships to enable our mission. It gave us the ability to strengthen other parts of the local economy without diluting our core focus on food and restaurants.

Empowering Local Small Businesses

Employee Appreciation

The pandemic and the government stimulus checks resulted in an unexpected outcome: labor shortages. This was particularly hard for restaurants. Working at a restaurant can be a grueling grind. The pandemic had forced people to pause and rethink their lives and reevaluate livelihoods. This, coupled with the cash infusion through stimulus checks, prompted restaurant workers to not return to work as the pandemic receded. This placed an immense strain on these local restaurants that were already struggling from the effects of the pandemic.

Essential Initiatives and Their Alignment

I started to explore ideas to help restaurants with their staffing situation. We wanted to reduce attrition and make our community more desirable for restaurant staff to come and be a part of. We wanted to make our local restaurant staff feel welcome and appreciated. This prompted the employee appreciation initiative. The concept was simple. Local nonfood small businesses would donate their products, services, or cash to Takeout 25, and Takeout 25 would use the products, services, or cash as gifts to restaurant employees nominated by local restaurant owners.

Through the month of January, we publicly appreciated the restaurant employees and acknowledged the local business sponsoring the gift with daily posts in the Takeout 25 group. In addition to appreciating the efforts of restaurant staff, this gave us an opportunity to promote nonfood businesses without diluting our focus on food. Once again, a win-win idea that has since become an annual effort every January as the restaurants ease into winter after a hectic holiday season.

RAVI'S FACEBOOK POST

JANUARY 10, 2022

Dear Takeout 25 family,

We are going to appreciate local restaurant staff throughout the month of January with gifts from sponsors who care about this community. If you run into these restaurant staff, take a moment to congratulate them. Show them that they are seen and their work is appreciated.

Today we recognize Yesenia Reyes from Cafe Cubano who receives a $100 gift certificate from Magical Minds Studio

THE TAKEOUT 25 EFFECT

> – Creative Development (Art Supplies) + $25 in gift cards from Sean Olis at Guaranteed Rate. Thanks, Hajjar Mohammed and Sean Olis.
>
> Here is what Mayra Fernandez, the owner, had to say about Yesenia: "I nominate my waitress Yesenia Reyes. She is a single mom and such a hard worker. Been with me over 7 years!"
>
> Congrats Yesenia! Your hard work is appreciated. Thanks.
> #takeout25
> #EmployeeAppreciation

Takeout 25 Holiday Gift Card Bundle

In November 2021, I was exploring ideas to combine food and gifts in a fun way that builds community during the holidays. Connie Brown, the owner of the Brown Cow Ice Cream Parlor, suggested exchanging $25 restaurant gift cards among restaurant owners to be gifted to restaurant staff. This would give restaurant staff more variety instead of just cards for the restaurants they work at. I took this idea and expanded it community wide.

In the Takeout 25 holiday gift card bundle, community members would buy $25 restaurant gift card bundles. The gift card bundles started from $25 and included $50, $75, $100, $150, and $250 bundles. The buyer of a bundle of gift cards did not get to choose specific gift cards in the bundle; they were randomly selected from the pool of available gift cards. This would give gift card recipients the opportunity to try food from local restaurants that they had not visited previously and support more of our local favorites in the process.

In four days, we set up our ticketing site and started collecting gift cards from restaurants. More than thirty restaurants participated in 2021, and we completely sold out of available gift cards.

Takeout 25 Embraces Spirit of the Season
Get Your Hands on Gift Card Bundles to Support Local Restaurants

by **Melissa Elsmo**, December 14, 2021

<small>This article was originally published in *Wednesday Journal* and appears here with permission.</small>

Takeout 25 is embracing the spirit of the season by applying its unique approach to supporting restaurants to holiday gift giving. Takeout 25 has created a program to bolster business at local eateries through the winter and a second to show appreciation for hardworking restaurant workers.

"It has been an especially rough year for restaurant workers, but it has also been hard on owners, too," said Ravi Parakkat, Takeout 25 founder and an Oak Park village trustee. "These programs help show appreciation for staff members, promote connectivity between restaurants, and encourage the community to support the industry as a whole."

Takeout 25 is offering "secret Santa" style gift card bundles in various amounts for community members to purchase. Sold in $25, $50, $100, and $250 bundles, the cards will offer a surprise assortment of $25 cards from more 40 participating restaurants in Oak Park, Forest Park, Austin, Berwyn and Elmwood Park. Thanks to the random nature of the bundles, participants may receive cards from restaurants they already know and love or may end up discovering a new place to dine.

"For each $25 card a restaurant contributes to the pre-sold bundles they will receive $25 in return," said Parakkat. "People can choose to donate separately to support future Takeout 25 events."

Visit www.givesignup.org/TicketEvent/TakeoutHoliday GiftCardBundles to make a purchase. Sales close on Friday, Dec. 17 at 5 p.m. Once purchased, gift cards will be available for pick up on Dec. 19 at Poke Burrito. To date, more than $7,500 in cards have been purchased. Parakkat is clear this first-time effort comes without expectations and considers any outcome to be great for the restaurant community and a learning opportunity for Takeout 25.

Takeout 25 is also using its platform to bring holiday cheer to hardworking restaurant workers. The same local restaurants are coming together to show their appreciation for their staff by pooling gift cards to distribute among local restaurant workers. Connie Ostler Brown, owner of The Brown Cow, Jimmy Chen, owner of Poke Burrito, and Kristen Alfonsi, co-owner of One Lake Brewing helped to shape the idea and planned its execution.

Community minded businesses like Delivery First ($750), Byline Bank ($500), Guaranteed Rate ($250) are sponsoring the program. The Carleton Hotel has donated a one-night stay to be raffled off to one lucky restaurant worker. Elements Massage and Mend Wellness (Oak Park) have donated massage sessions and Ahimsa Yoga Studio, Magical Minds Studio and Dark Matter Coffee have also made contributions to the effort.

"Everyone involved is really excited," said Parakkat. "After coming up with the idea, it took just four days to

Essential Initiatives and Their Alignment

> launch the program. It took everyone by surprise, but people are very excited. This is a positive effort that enables the economy in a new innovative way."

In the second installment of the holiday gift card event, we kept the concept the same, and once again, it was a resounding success. In addition to gift card purchases, residents could donate to Takeout 25 so that we were able to fulfill our mission. This time, we received an unexpected donation from a generous resident, Marina Mondello. She then wanted to match every dollar donated by other community members. This prompted more community members to donate. Takeout 25 had the opportunity to use these extra donations to support local individuals and families in need.

I reached out to David Pope, the executive director of the Residence Corporation and a former mayor of Oak Park, to see if we could support families in the housing voucher program that the Oak Park Residence Corporation was responsible for administering. David agreed to facilitate the gifting, and we used the donations to buy restaurant gift cards and gifted them to 141 families in our community. Thus, by sheer chance and Marina's generosity, we were able to leverage the holiday gift card program to serve our food security mission.

Takeout 25 Owners/Managers Meetups

As I shared in chapter 4, Takeout 25 organized the first in-person owners/managers meetup at Taco Mucho in April 2022. We've had two more since.

In April 2022, we agreed to meet every six months. I had seen several small business events that were organized based on the organizers' convenience and not focused on the participants. I wanted to change that. We picked a Sunday evening 6:00 to 9:00 p.m. in October and Monday 6:00 to 9:00 p.m. in April, as these were the times and days that most restaurant owners preferred.

We wanted the first hour to be used productively, so we set it up like a workshop from my consulting days. We split up into three groups, and each group was tasked with brainstorming ideas in one of the three buckets:

- Increase revenue
- Reduce cost
- Foster collaboration

The participants could each select the group they wanted to be a part of. Each group, in addition to brainstorming ideas that contributed to the theme, had to prioritize the top two ideas. Each group had thirty minutes, and the group's discussion was facilitated by a Takeout 25 board member. After the group was done with brainstorming and prioritization, one person from each group had to present their group's results to the broader group. We spent fifteen minutes hearing each other's reports. We then placed the two prioritized ideas from each group up on the wall (total of six ideas). We gave each participant three dot stickers and invited them to vote their preference by sticking a dot next to the ideas they liked and would like to collectively spend time executing. They had the entire evening to consider and discuss the options with the other participants and place their vote. It was a huge success, with several excellent ideas generated. At the end of the evening at each meetup, ideas would be prioritized for execution. Some examples include:

- Consolidation of credit card processing to reduce processing fees
- Bulk purchasing of sustainable packaging to make it more affordable
- Positioning us as Illinois's first green dining hub
- Takeout 25 boxed water marketing

I'll talk about these ideas and their execution in more detail in the rest of this chapter.

Credit Card Payment Processing

The more I thought about ways to help small locally owned restaurants, the more I was convinced that collective action can unlock new value for these small businesses. They are often so consumed by their own business that it's difficult to explore collective action or collaboration. Takeout 25 had brought these small businesses together. Now, would we be able to facilitate collective action? The ideas prioritized at the first owners meetup seemed to suggest that the owners were ready to move in this direction.

We wanted to test the concept of collective action but did not want to start with a complex use case. We had to pick a project that offered tangible monetary value but did not have physical complexity. So we decided to focus on the less complex financial transaction—reducing credit card processing fees through collective contracting—as the test case instead of taking on the inherent complexity of a physical transaction, like bulk purchasing of packaging material.

I reached out to a few financial institutions to explore options. The credit card processing fee structure was intentionally opaque. Every conversation helped me fully understand why these small businesses were struggling with this topic. There was the interchange rate. The different card providers charged their fee over this base interchange rate. So the fee was different for different card providers. To make matters worse, it was also different for different cards they offered. Then there was the equipment fee, batching fee, integration with the point-of-sale system, etc. It was a dizzying array of options, and this made the charges very difficult to comprehend. So most small businesses would just pay the bill without challenging it.

A local couple who were part of Takeout 25 owned a payment processing company, Tidal Commerce. I reached out to them and was able to cut through the complexity to create a simple agreement with two options, one for new businesses needing a lower negotiated base rate (fixed model) and the other for a more established business that needed to lower existing fees (variable model). It's early days, but we now have a couple of local restaurants signed up through the arrangement.

Recurring Events: Taste the Town and Barrie Fest

Earlier in the book, I shared how events became a part of Takeout 25's economic empowerment arsenal. Our signature event, Taste the Town, started virtually during the pandemic and has now become an annual in-person event where we bring food, entertainment, music, tourism, etc. to promote our community as a destination.

Essential Initiatives and Their Alignment

Taste the Town events were a joy to cover—they combined dishes from multiple local restaurants into one delicious experience. Early Taste the Town events were served up drive-through style, while later iterations were held in person with live music and loads of face-to-face interaction. Each raised significant dollars for local organizations all while supporting restaurants, minimizing waste, and building community.

As I enjoyed a noteworthy surf and turf cup at the first in-person Taste the Town event in June 2022, I looked around and realized Ravi and his team had successfully brought the virtual world of Takeout 25 to life as supporters enjoyed a meal together for the first time.
—**MELISSA ELSMO**, food editor, *Wednesday Journal* (Growing Community Media)

In 2023, the Taste the Town event was even bigger than 2022. Each year, we experienced a steady increase in ticketed participants. The common factor in both of the in-person Taste the Town events has been the venue FitzGerald's, an iconic music venue located in Berwyn, a Takeout 25 community.

After our launch as a not-for-profit at the 2021 Barrie Fest, we have partnered with SEOPCO on two more Barrie Fests. Once again, we've been able to expand participation at the event by providing a diverse set of food options. In the 2023 edition, we launched our community as Illinois's first green dining hub.

One-Time Event: Dining in Our Community – Past, Present, and Future

In the spring of 2023, we partnered with the local history museum to curate a food-focused panel discussion, Dining in Our Community – Past, Present, and Future. This was an intimate ticketed event hosted at the museum. The museum director, Frank Lipo, and museum board president, Frances Knechel, provided the historical context while five local restaurant owners with diverse backgrounds and experiences discussed the dining scene, how it has evolved, and what the future might hold. In addition to moderating the panel, I highlighted that positioning our community as Illinois's first green dining hub provides a compelling vision for the future that truly differentiates us.

The audience enjoyed the panel discussion, and I learned a thing or two about local dining from the restaurant owners and the museum staff.

Tackling Food Insecurity

The Takeout 25 service territory is composed of communities with significant socioeconomic disparities. I expected the unaddressed food needs to be significant in the Austin neighborhood of Chicago and less so in an affluent community like Oak Park. I quickly realized that this is an incorrect assumption. Even in an affluent community like Oak Park, there were food needs that remain woefully unaddressed. I was particularly surprised when I started getting direct messages from community members once they heard about Takeout 25's mission to address food insecurity. Many of the people who reached out lived in large homes on the north side of the village, typically considered the more affluent part of the community. What I discovered was that there are several families that have inherited large homes but do not have the means to be food secure. So a family may look well-situated based on where they live, but the reality may be quite different. I would have never seen this side of the community if not for pursuing the local food security as a mission through Takeout 25.

I approached the tactical requests that I received in two ways:
- I directed folks to other partner agencies and resources available within our community.
- I also started maintaining a stash of restaurant gift cards that I could hand out as immediate short-term help.

It's always heartbreaking to realize the magnitude of the need and one person's total inability to meet that need. All you can hope is to make the situation better for at least a few.

Enabling Our Partners Focused on Addressing Food Insecurity

The intention of adding food security into the Takeout 25 mission was very specific. Through my efforts on Takeout 25 during the pandemic, I had witnessed food waste and food need coexist in our community. Through Takeout 25, we wanted to explore how to bridge the gap between food waste and food need in our own unique way. We also wanted to enable other entities that were already addressing this space, while not simply replicating their efforts. Through our events, we started to raise funds for entities in the space such as Beyond Hunger (the local food pantry) and Austin Coming Together (Austin Eats). This was particularly true for Barrie Fest since it was organized in September (Hunger Action Month). We would partner with one of these local not-for-profits and raise funds for their efforts.

THE TAKEOUT 25 EFFECT

In 2022, Anthony Clark, a local community organizer, reached out to me. Anthony had set up community fridges locally to address food insecurity. People could place food in these fridges, and anybody was welcome to take what they needed (no questions asked). I liked the idea and genuinely wanted it to succeed. He wanted me to engage the Takeout 25 restaurants to see if they could help stock the fridges with food (especially protein). I was concerned about our collective inexperience in physically handling food. This had community health implications and needed specialized expertise to execute safely. I shared my concern with Anthony, and we agreed to engage Beyond Hunger. Beyond Hunger agreed to train our volunteers on food handling.

However, the whole plan fizzled out as everyone got busy. The next thing I heard is that a couple of local locations, Oak Park Main Library and Carnival Grocery, had to be closed. I'm not sure exactly where the initiative stands at this point, but I do believe that the core idea still has a lot of promise and want to acknowledge Anthony's work as its architect locally.

Food for Warming Shelter

A substantial benefit of the Takeout 25 Owners/Managers Network came when we were offered the opportunity to give back to our own community. As winter began, two overnight shelters for unhoused people were opening in Oak Park. The shelters reached out to Takeout 25 for dinners and breakfasts for these guests. Ravi responded by asking the group to help as they were able. He did fundraising from the community to support this work. We had a

system in place to manage this work. I remember my crew making the first dinner. They were young people who felt the joy of connection in preparing the meal and packing it—they put a lot of love in those boxes. This effort was continued for a second winter, and I believe it is here to stay.
—MICHELLE MASCARO, owner, Happy Apple Pie Shop

John Harris, who serves on the Takeout 25 board, also leads and facilitates the efforts of the Oak Park Homelessness Coalition (OPHC). He came to me with a request in January 2022: Could Takeout 25 organize food for an emergency shelter that the OPHC was setting up in partnership with Housing Forward and other community partners? While this did not directly fit into what we had done until that point, I was keen to address food insecurity locally. So I decided to closely examine this unique challenge for the opportunity to create a win-win solution.

After much thought and several conversations, we came up with a model with a role for every stakeholder:

- Restaurants would sign up with Takeout 25 to provide subsidized meals (breakfast or dinner) that would still bring in revenue during lean winter months and cover their costs.
- We arranged for the food to be picked up and delivered pro bono by a local delivery service (Delivery First).
- We raised funds from the community to pay the restaurants for the food so that the community could participate in the model on a voluntary basis to address a problem they cared about.

- Housing Forward volunteers coordinated the efforts at the shelter.
- Community organizations (Rush Hospital, churches, etc.) provided the space for the shelters.
- Oak Park Homelessness Coalition and Village of Oak Park Emergency response teams provided coordination and facilitation support.

Our initial intent was to run this program for six weeks on a trial basis, though we extended it to eight weeks, based on need, the success of the model, and the community support that enabled that success. Over eight weeks, we delivered over fifteen hundred meals to the shelters. We repeated this model in 2023 with similar impact, and it aligns with two of our three mission elements: empowering local restaurants while addressing food insecurity.

Reinventing Nonprofits, Restaurants Team with Rush Warming Center

Broad Collaboration Brings Breakfast and Dinner to Rush Oak Park Warming Center

by **Melissa Elsmo**, January 25, 2022

<small>This article was originally published in *Wednesday Journal* and appears here with permission.</small>

Rush Oak Park Hospital has transformed its former Emergency Department into a 24/7 warming center at 610 S. Maple Ave. A collaboration between a trio of nonprofits and a bevy of local restaurants is bringing breakfast and dinner to guests seeking shelter from the cold.

"Housing Forward, the Oak Park Homelessness Coalition, and the Village of Oak Park have had a relationship for many years. Rush Oak Park and West Suburban Hospital were easy additions to our existing collaboration," said Lynda Schueler, executive director of Housing Forward. "Rush's warming center is open 24/7 so adding a meal program there made sense to us. We expect the meal program to expand organically, and we are open to including West Sub if they see a need."

John Harris, coordinator of the Oak Park Homelessness Coalition, reached out to Ravi Parakkat, a village trustee and Takeout 25 founder, to ask if the organization would have an interest in coordinating meals for the center. Parakkat was enthused at the prospect of using the non-profit to assist with the program.

"We reached out to Takeout 25 community members to back the cause and they generously donated $8,500 to keep the meal program cost neutral for restaurants providing meals," said Parakkat. "Restaurant owners were quick to sign up to help. We actually had more takers than we needed and have a few restaurants on standby."

Takeout 25's trial program is expected to run for six weeks providing breakfast and dinner Monday through Thursday for an average of 12 guests. Delivery First, a local delivery company, has stepped up to transport the meals at no cost and the community donations fully cover the costs for six weeks of meals sourced through Takeout 25 based on an allotment of $75 per day for breakfast and $150 per day for dinner. Housing Forward separately

THE TAKEOUT 25 EFFECT

acquired a grant to provide meals between Friday and Sunday and intend to rely on existing restaurant partnerships to facilitate the weekend program. The warming center at Rush is open when temperatures dip below freezing and has a maximum capacity of 15 people with social distancing protocols in place.

The program launched last week with Joana Fischer of Twisted Cookie, 7401 Madison St., Forest Park, providing apple pie cookies for the inaugural breakfast and Josh Darr of local start-up Darr-B-Q serving a hearty meal of smoked brisket and almond pear cobbler for the kick-off dinner. Fischer said she jumped on board because she is inspired by Parakkat's ongoing efforts to support local restaurants and Darr said participating felt like "the next right thing to do."

Oak Park's Poke Burrito, Eastgate Café and Happy Apple Pie Shop also provided meals during the first week of the program.

"The food community is so generous," said Michelle Mascaro, owner of Happy Apple, 226 Harrison St. "Everybody is worthy of a meal. Good food, made with love, makes a real difference in people's lives."

Mascaro, who provided warm spinach quiche and fresh oranges for breakfast last week, notes that supporting the warming center is personal to her. She has a former employee who deals with complex mental health issues and grapples with homelessness. He is often a guest at Rush's warming center.

"This is the first time we've done anything like this," said Schueler. "People using the center have been extremely grateful for the meals."

Essential Initiatives and Their Alignment

In the coming weeks the Oak Park based program is scheduled to receive support from Two Sisters Restaurant and Catering located in Chicago's Austin neighborhood.

"Food should not only be for people who can afford it," said Veah Larde, chef owner of Two Sisters, 4800 W. Chicago Ave. "Why not help someone? Most people are a moment away from needing help — needing help to pay a bill, find some heat or get a meal."

In 2020, the pandemic forced Housing Forward to close the 24-hour overnight shelter it had operated for 29 years in the community. The pause in the shelter program created a "hole of need" according to Harris and forced the organizations to develop a "two-pronged approach" to fill the service gap and combat issues of homelessness during the winter.

Schueler and Harris credit Michael Montino, the village government's emergency preparedness coordinator, and fresh leadership at both Rush and West Sub, for helping to clarify ways they could meet the needs of people who do not have access to heat. In addition to promoting the five warming centers located inside Oak Park's libraries and hospitals, they have developed a program with support from faith community leaders that triggers the opening of emergency overnight shelters in churches in the event of an extended winter weather event.

"The partnership with Ravi, Takeout 25 and the local restaurant community drove up awareness about our local warming centers," said Harris. "Community collaboration is necessary if you are going to change the world."

Commitment to Sustainability

Sustainability as a mission element for Takeout 25 was important for me. As I was transitioning from corporate life to public service, I was convinced that the world would increasingly be viewed through two lenses: digital technology and environmental sustainability. My corporate career in digital transformation had morphed into my work in digital transformation with Junior Achievement of Chicago. I had a broad and holistic view of the evolving digital ecosystem, and Junior Achievement provided the opportunity to exercise my consulting skills to harness the transformative power of digital technologies to have a significant impact. I wanted to do more in sustainability.

As I was shaping the future of Takeout 25, I wanted to make sure we would address local food-related sustainability in our own unique way. Takeout 25 encouraged community members to buy takeout food to support restaurants during the pandemic. Takeout food resulted in plastic waste, and we wanted to rectify that situation. So, through partnerships with the local chapter of Clean Up – Give Back, we started getting involved in plastic collection drives. Clean Up – Give Back had a board composed of mostly local high-schoolers. Their volunteer base would help manage events sustainably by sorting waste streams from an event. These volunteers also took on projects to collect and segregate plastic waste and recycle it. Takeout 25 used its social media reach in the community to help raise awareness and enable collection efforts. We also partnered with Clean Up – Give Back to manage our events sustainably. We first worked together at the Takeout 25 NFP launch event at Barrie Fest in 2021 and have worked together since.

The kids from Clean Up – Give Back collected twenty-two hundred pounds of plastic and sent them to a program with Trex, a plastic upcycling company. These plastics were consolidated at the local Jewel-Osco grocery store and sent to Trex. For every five hundred pounds of plastic collected, Trex would give an upcycled plastic bench in return. Takeout 25 organized for the bench to be donated back to the community through the local library. The bench was placed in the lobby of the Oak Park Main Library as a physical symbol of the community's shared journey during the pandemic.

A Symbol of Sustainability
Clean Up Give Back Partners with Takeout 25 to Install Library Bench
by **Melissa Elsmo**, November 16, 2021

This article was originally published in *Wednesday Journal* and appears here with permission.

On Nov. 15, in the lobby of the Oak Park Public Library Main Branch, 834 Lake St., a quartet of Oak Park and River Forest High School students unveiled a dark green bench made from upcycled plastics.

David Seleb, executive director of the Oak Park Public Library, was on site to welcome the bench donated by Clean Up Give Back, Takeout 25 and the Village of Oak Park. A plaque on the bench says, "Supporting our restaurants, upcycling our plastic, building a sustainable community."

"We really didn't know what we were getting into," said Aubrey Johnston, Clean Up Give Back member, holding up a garbage bag. "This bag of plastic weighs 3.7 pounds. We collected 40,000 of these to get to the 500 pounds we needed to earn this bench."

The students are members of the Oak Park chapter of Clean Up Give Back, a Des Plaines based non-profit dedicated to building communities through environmental stewardship. Under the mentorship of Oak Park resident Adrienne Eyer, the student-led group joined forces with the Interfaith Green Network and accepted the NexTrex "plastic film recycling challenge." Plastic film includes grocery bags, newspaper sleeves, bubble wrap and sandwich bags among others. Working in partnership with big box stores like Jewel Osco, NexTrex transforms film plastics into eco-conscious decking and challenges others to help support their work by increasing their plastic flow.

"In order to earn a bench, these students needed to collect 500 pounds of plastic film," said Eyer. "We were told it would take six months to reach that goal, but they ended up collecting 2,200 pounds in 12 weeks. This bench is a testament to these kids and this community."

The students managed collection boxes in several locations where residents could deposit qualifying film plastics. The receptacles were emptied, and contents were delivered to the River Forest Jewel, 7525 Lake St., to be shipped to Trex. There are clear rules in place that prohibit plastic donations from accumulating in the entryway areas of participating big box stores, but plastics came in so furiously that the store manager gave the group access to the loading dock to house the plastics — Eyer considers the Jewel staff to be the "heroes behind this project."

The students were overwhelmed by community support for the project and wanted the bench to be placed in a public space where it could be used and appreciated by the community. The students also recognize the

Essential Initiatives and Their Alignment

pandemic has increased the use of single-use plastics in the form of grocery bags and takeout food packaging. They reached out to Ravi Parakkat, Oak Park village trustee and Takeout 25 founder, in hopes he could use the momentum of Takeout 25 to help find a permanent home for the bench.

"Members of the Takeout 25 community have expressed concern about our increased use of single use plastics in the last year and it has been a sore point for me, too because I care deeply about these issues." said Parakkat. "We want to support local restaurants and we also want a sustainable community." Parakkat noted it took one call to the library to secure a spot for the bench.

"I think this is the perfect place for the bench and we are honored to have it here," said Seleb to the students. "One of the four strategic priorities at the library is stewardship so this fits in perfectly with the work the Oak Park Public Library is committed to doing in the community."

The next project we collaborated on was to collect #2 and #5 plastics for a local artist, Cody Norman. Cody makes art from plastic waste at his workshop. He was commissioned by the Chicago Botanic Garden to create a large art installation for their 50th anniversary celebrations in 2022. Together, Takeout 25 and CUGB collected and delivered the plastic required for Cody's work on this project. Cody create "Plasticus Porticus" that was exhibited at the Garden during the 2022 season.

Oak Park Artist Transforms Used Plastic into Work of Art

Cody Norman's "Plasticus Porticus," Made from Waste and with Help from Takeout 25, at Chicago Botanic Garden through September

by **Samantha Callender**, July 14, 2022

This article was originally published in *Austin Weekly News* and appears here with permission.

During the pandemic, Takeout 25 was created to help support local restaurants in Oak Park that were struggling to stay in business. The initiative, which started as neighbors helping neighbors, eventually turned into an organization that is still around today

Recently, Takeout 25 inspired an art installation at the Chicago Botanic Garden. Oak Park artist Cody Norman's "Plasticus Porticus" sculpture is made entirely of waste from takeout containers and was created by Norman in his studio at 5339 W. Lake Street in Austin.

"I started working with plastics in graduate school," said Norman. "Only 10% of plastic gets recycled, so I enjoy exploring how my work can recycle and tie back to these conversations of environmental consciousness and sustainability."

Oak Park Trustee Ravi Parakkat, founder of Takeout 25 and the organization's board president, said Norman's work is a representation of both the past and the future of Takeout 25.

The organization's projects fall under at least one of three core pillars: helping local businesses, addressing food security and sustainability.

"The connection that supporting businesses had with waste from takeout containers bothered me a little bit," said Parakkat. "This was a way to address that sustainability pillar."

"Plasticus Porticus" features a vibrant 12-foot arch that Norman created using a combination of high-density polyethylene and polypropylene plastics.

Norman used more than 250 pounds of the material for his work, which he describes as "a small-scale effort that can lead to larger changes in how individuals in our community choose to consume single-use plastic."

In collaboration with Oak Park and River Forest High School's Clean Up Give Back student group, Takeout 25 and Norman collected waste from area homes.

The piece will sit in residence at the Chicago Botanic Garden through September to commemorate the 50th anniversary of the gardens. Parakkat said he hopes the sculpture can find a permanent home in Austin, where it was created.

While the studio where Norman works isn't open to the public, he makes it a personal priority to engage with the neighborhood around him.

"I try to speak to folks and engage with them if they ask me what's going on around here," he said. "Folks have asked me what goes on in here and I tell them there's a bunch of artists in there creating things. They tell me stories of racing go karts around the building when it was abandoned. I've learned so much about the history of this block from the residents."

Parakkat said Takeout 25 wants to engage more with the Austin community and encourages small businesses in Austin to join their network.

"We want to break down the lines that exist with Austin. We're always interested in the impact versus our intent," Parakkat said. "Our members share everything from resources to professional connections and just general advice. We'd really like for Austin business owners to be in on this as well."

Residents organized plastic collection drives on the Takeout 25 Facebook group.

I used the Takeout 25 FB forum to organize four collections of plastic takeout containers in 2021 and 2022. This happened after I noticed lots of people posting about "What do I do with all this plastic?" I set up a collection bin at St. Christopher's Church in south Oak Park and regularly updated people on the Takeout 25 thread. I collected plastic every day for two weeks. Most of it went to two places—Housing Forward and the Way Back Inn (in Maywood).
—**PAUL CLARK**, Oak Park resident

While recycling plastic was a worthy goal, there was more created every day, and we wanted to do something to replace plastic use in the community. This aspiration has since shaped our sustainability journey. We created a Takeout 25 branded boxed water to replace plastic water bottles with paper, and we embarked on a journey to position our community as Illinois's first green dining hub.

Takeout 25 Boxed Water

I drank my first box of water at Langham Hotel in Chicago in the fall of 2021. I was aware of boxed water through my conversations

Essential Initiatives and Their Alignment

with the founder of Just Water earlier that year, but until I stayed at Langham, I had never held a box of water in my hand or consumed its contents. This experience got me to connect the dots in my head. I took the empty box of water from Langham home. I wanted to use boxed water as a replacement for plastic water bottles in the Takeout 25 service territory. I wanted to create a Takeout 25 branded boxed water. I was also thinking of additional ways to deliver more value to the community through this product. I decided to include a QR code in the water box. The QR code would be the access point to a dynamic digital experience that can be refreshed without having to change the physical product design. The digital experience we designed consolidated local dining specials and offers to make them easy and convenient to access for community members buying the boxed water. By bringing the digital and physical aspects of the water box together, we could simultaneously replace plastic water bottles while enabling local businesses by promoting their specials.

I connected with the water box manufacturer, WaterBox LLC, and decided to move forward with an order in February 2022. From the time we placed the order, it would take three to four months to deliver the product. I was hoping to have the boxes delivered by September 2022 in time for 2022 Barrie Fest, marking the first anniversary of Takeout 25's launch as a not-for-profit. So we did not have a lot of time to design the product and place the order.

I worked with Takeout 25 board member John Harris's team at a5 Inc. for a preliminary design. We then leveraged the design capabilities available through WaterBox LLC. This was a huge help, as they fully understood how the design would translate to the box when manufactured.

I was very happy with their design, which also included the QR code, and we finalized the design and placed the initial order in April 2022. While the order was to be delivered by late August, the supply chain delays caused by the pandemic and printing bottlenecks delayed the order until March 2023. So, from concept to product delivery, it took about eighteen months.

We decided to soft-launch the product in March 2023 at a local grocery store (Carnival Grocery) and then formally launched it on Earth Day (April 22). In the initial four months since launch, we replaced twelve thousand plastic bottles in our community. The Takeout 25 boxed water is now available in thirty-three locations locally, including grocery stores, gyms, hospitals, apartment complexes, and restaurants. We partnered with a small local distributor, Montrose Wholesale, to store and distribute the boxed water. We are in the early stages of this product, and while the early signs are encouraging, there is much to be learned and implemented as we move forward.

While the community was largely supportive, the product launch was not without its share of criticism. Some questioned whether this product was truly sustainable, and others questioned my motives behind the launch of this product. While some of these critics were coming from a genuine wish to understand the details, there were others who were more against me than the product itself. We had to pay close attention to every criticism to make sure we were not ignoring important feedback that could help improve the product. Some folks took the opportunity to raise concerns about other core Takeout 25 principles. With us still growing quickly, I wanted to make sure I addressed these concerns comprehensively, not just for the folks raising the concerns but also for others in the group. I also wanted to isolate these discussions into a single thread. The criticisms and attacks subsided in a few days once I presented all the facts in a post to directly address the concerns raised.

We now have John Mastrodonato, an MBA student at Dominican University, interning with us to do a market assessment for Takeout 25 boxed water to help us evaluate the key sales and distribution channels to meet local demand.

Addressing Community Concerns

It's often difficult to determine genuine concerns and criticism versus malicious ones. It's important that organizations focused on social change and impact address the concerns raised by the community in a comprehensive and transparent way. I'm sharing a Facebook post from shortly after the launch of the Takeout 25 boxed water initiative.

RAVI'S FACEBOOK POST

APRIL 28, 2023

Dear Takeout 25 family,

   Several questions have come up in the group as we grow bigger and more removed from our origins. Most of them are some flavor of "Why do we do what we do?" Through this post, I wanted to get everyone in the group up to speed on our evolution and its rationale. Warning: This is a long post. Takeout 25 started as a Facebook group in 2020 November to help local restaurants survive the pandemic by bringing the community together with an emphasis on positivity. We grew quickly and made a difference in the community through our collective efforts. We grew in an inclusive manner by welcoming all the neighboring communities around Oak Park into the Takeout 25 network. We expanded our activities into events (Takeout 25 Taste the Town, Takeout 25 holiday gift card bundle, etc.) to further build community and support local restaurants. (We now have 12,600 members.)

With the pandemic receding in 2021, rather than killing the group, we decided to pivot and set it up as a local not-for-profit 501(c)(6), Takeout 25 NFP. We expanded the mission to include sustainability and food security. This expanded our activities into plastic collection for art, providing food for the winter warming shelter and partnerships with other impactful not-for-profits benefiting several social causes.

Our main revenue source was events (60%), large contributions (30%), and small donations (10%) from generous community members (0 grants, 0 public funding, or 0 membership fee). Until we set up the not-for-profit, everything we raised would directly flow through to participating restaurants and not-for-profit partners. Once we set up the not-for-profit, we incurred some (less than 5% of our revenue) administrative costs (e.g., compliance, accounting fee, filing fee, legal fee, technology subscriptions). Now, with the boxed water, we are diversifying our revenue options to have a bigger impact with our mission (e.g., promoting our community as Illinois's first green dining hub). Our activities are getting more complex, and we do not have a single full-time or part-time paid employee. We have a great crew of volunteers,

Essential Initiatives and Their Alignment

administrators, contractors, interns, board members, and partners who believe in what we are doing together.

I'm writing the response below to the questions raised in the group over this past year so that we can all point people to this post for future reference as these questions pop up. We'll add to this or clarify as appropriate over time.

Why can't we share negative experiences on Takeout 25?
Takeout 25 is a positive space on social media, and we would like to keep it that way. What we are suggesting is shift the scale of your feedback from negative to positive (e.g., -5 to +5) to zero to positive (e.g., 0 to 10). You don't have to say anything negative when you have a bad experience. Your silence about a local establishment can speak volumes without getting negative.

Why is Takeout 25 deleting my comments?
We do this when and only when a group rule that was agreed to at the time of joining the group was broken (e.g., the positivity rule).

Why are you NOT allowing posts about non-brick-and-mortar food places?
Brick-and-mortar businesses in our view require a level of financial investment in our community that others do not. Their cost structure and risk profile reflect this, and hence they need more support. We are constantly evaluating when and how we may be able to expand our support, but for now, we would rather remain focused.

Why are you NOT allowing posts about corporate chains that have local ownership?
Corporate chains (international, national, multistate, etc.) have the advantage of umbrella marketing that independent small businesses do not. We do support small local chains, but we avoid large corporate chains to help level the playing field.

Why are GoFundMe posts not allowed on Takeout 25?
Once we start allowing them, its going to be very difficult for us to moderate the group. On rare occasions, the admin group decides to let one through (after much discussion) if it is consistent with our mission, but that is entirely at the group admin/moderator's discretion.

Why is Takeout 25 selling boxed water? Is it recyclable? Where is the money from it going?
The Takeout 25 boxed water is more sustainable than plastic water bottles, and if you scan the QR code on the box with your phone, it takes you to a website where we have consolidated local dining specials. So, with this initiative, we are addressing local sustainability and economic empowerment of restaurants (two important elements of our mission). The goal is to only replace plastic water bottle use in our community. If you use reusable containers to drink tap water, then please continue to do so. This water is not for you. Ultimately, in most things, the most sustainable option would be to reduce consumption and eliminate waste (including packaging waste) to the extent possible.

The boxed water is 100% recyclable and is on the approved list from our local waste hauler LRS. You can contact them at 844-NEED-LRS for any additional details.

Setting up a new consumer product is a complicated affair. We are in the early stages of the product's evolution, and we are still figuring out the cost structure and how to manage the pricing structure and distribution to meet the cost. Having said that, any money we make as a not-for-profit will be used entirely to work on our mission. Once the level of this activity grows beyond a point, then we may have to look at how to handle it to meet legal and compliance requirements. Some activities may not fit within the not-for-profit 501(c)(6) status in the long run. We have a legal team working on helping us figure that out so that we can plan and prepare for our next financial year starting July 1, 2023.

How do I look up the financials for Takeout 25 NFP?
Takeout 25 NFP is a 501(c)(6) not-for-profit incorporated in Illinois. We have to annually file our financial reports (990) with the IRS (federal) and IL Attorney General's office (state), and these are available for public access. We have also consistently posted the financials of events and initiatives hosted by us in the Takeout 25 group for visibility and transparency.

If you have additional questions, would like to see how we operate, or be a part of what we are doing, the door is always open for you to come help out as a volunteer. Thank you! #takeout25

Green Dining Hub

Post-pandemic recovery has been robust in our community with new business license applications hitting record highs in 2021 and 2022. We had attracted many restaurateurs to come invest in and be a part of our community. Some of them openly acknowledge that one of the key reasons for their choice of location was the presence of Takeout 25. They knew we had been able to mobilize the community at scale to support local restaurants. This fueled our ambitions, and we wanted to do more to promote our community as a destination.

We have some great restaurants and restaurant owners in our area, and I really wanted to start positioning our community as a dining destination. I knew it would be difficult to compete, based on food quality and variety, with the diverse options available close by in the foodie city of Chicago. This prompted me initially to look at combining local dining experiences with the tourism that we have locally (Frank Lloyd Wright Home and Studio, Ernest Hemingway's birthplace, etc.) to attract people to our community.

This was in 2022, when most communities were trying to figure out how to facilitate economic recovery from the pandemic, and rising inflation presented a serious threat. The stimulus checks that helped people navigate the pandemic created excess liquidity resulting in this inflation. The conflict in Ukraine pushed fossil fuel prices up and made inflation worse. This, coupled with supply chain disruptions and geopolitical unrest, created an environment that forced central banks to take drastic action to tame inflation.

Local communities were not immune to these macroeconomic factors but could do very little about them. Local restaurants were stuck between the rising cost of ingredients and their inability to pass that cost to customers. Takeout 25 had to evaluate what we could do locally to help this situation.

In late summer 2022, I was introduced to Cassie Carroll from Smart Energy Design Assistance Center (SEDAC) at the University of Illinois in Champaign-Urbana. SEDAC runs the Illinois Green Business Program and was working with the Village of Oak Park to provide some assistance with the Oak Park Climate Action Plan.

In my introductory call with Cassie, I shared my aspiration to position our community as a dining destination. We then discussed green dining, and this ultimately led to us considering the possibility of building Illinois's first green dining hub in the Takeout 25 community. I left that call excited and over the next few days thought through the idea. I was convinced that if a green dining hub concept could work in Illinois, it had to be in a community like ours where both the residents and the businesses were open and willing to adopt sustainability practices. If an entity could facilitate this, it would be Takeout 25, with its commitment to the economic success of local restaurants and sustainability.

Being Illinois's first green dining hub also provided a way to differentiate our local dining and added one more reason for people to come be a part of our community.

Sustainability often represents a cost (more expensive compostable containers, for example), and for small business owners, anything that increases their operating costs is a scary proposition. While I wanted to green our local food businesses, I wanted to do this in a commercially responsible way. This was nonnegotiable for me. We presented the concept to the restaurant owners in the Takeout 25 network at the owners/managers meetup in October 2022. The participating restaurants were excited about the concept and gave us the support required to move forward. So, with support from local restaurants and technical expertise from committed partner SEDAC, we embarked on the journey to set up Illinois's first green dining hub: Takeout 25 Green Dining Hub.

Cassie and team then assessed a representative set of local businesses that included coffee shops, pubs, wine merchants, sit-down restaurants, fast-food joints, and even a cooperative grocery store. The goal of these assessments was to identify:

- Actions that were already successfully implemented and help share them more broadly with the community
- Strategies that restaurants needed to implement individually based on their unique circumstances
- Strategies that could be executed collectively to make it easier and cost-effective

We presented and discussed the results from these early assessments at the April 2023 owners meetup. Through that discussion, we set the formal launch of the hub for late summer 2023. We wanted to have twenty-five restaurants (25% of the Takeout 25's network) participating in the initial launch. We ended up with twenty-eight participants for the launch.

As far as helping the community understand the concept, Takeout 25 and SEDAC coauthored a position paper to explain it. Once again, Melissa Elsmo covered the announcement and our plans for the green dining hub in her *Wednesday Journal* article and Mike Stephen interviewed me on his WGN radio show *Outside the Loop*.

We brought on Zoharia Drizin as an intern to help support our efforts. She grew up in Oak Park and was pursuing her masters in sustainability management at DePaul University. She was tasked with recruiting and training community ambassadors for the green dining hub. She also assisted Cassie with the restaurant assessments and analysis.

We wanted the Takeout 25 Green Dining Hub to be the first in Illinois, but we did not want it to be the last or only one in Illinois. We wanted to create an identity for the hub that was independent of but complementary to the Takeout 25 and SEDAC brands. Once again, John Harris's a5 Inc. team stepped in to help create marketing assets to support the launch of the green dining hub, including a logo. As I write this book, we have the green dining hub launched. I am excited to see how this effort evolves and spreads over the coming months and years.

In the fifteen years of working with businesses across Illinois to reduce environmental impact, this is the first group of restaurants that has such a deep commitment both to its community and interest in sustainability. Takeout 25 has built trust with restaurant owners through the work it did to support and amplify restaurants during the pandemic. They helped many restaurant owners save their businesses by promoting takeout to the community. Takeout 25 saved many families' livelihoods, helping more owners and staff members feed their families or pay their rent. This builds a deep level of respect, trust, and relationship between restaurants and the organization.

Without this type of trust and sharing common goals, collaboration around sustainability initiatives would not be possible. Restaurant owners are responding to customer demand for sustainability, such

THE TAKEOUT 25 EFFECT

as using compostable to-go containers or recycling waste. They want to do more but need help to go further. I wish more communities in Illinois had the consumer demand that this region does. Restaurants that are willing to work together to seek solutions to better serve their customers, the community, and the environment. I first collaborated with Takeout 25 because of their alignment around sustainability. I then partnered with them to build Illinois's first green dining hub because of the owners. They all work together to achieve common goals through collaboration, creativity, and knowledge-sharing. Takeout 25 brought together people who rarely have time to connect and created a place to help businesses thrive. I knew that Takeout 25 was the organization to launch something special, and I am thrilled by the enthusiasm of the owners to take on sustainability.

—**CASSIE CARROLL**, SEDAC marketing and outreach program director

KEY TAKEAWAYS

- Understand how you can uniquely add value to your mission elements. Replication of tried-and-tested models is not exciting and often not impactful either.

- Use every event and initiative as an opportunity to innovate.

- A movement is about people. Be sure to not lose your people. Bring them along at every initiative and event.

- Start small with available resources. Scale is not as important as relevance.

- Always focus on and measure the impact of your initiatives.

- Communicate the impact, and if community funds are involved, communicate how they're getting deployed. Transparency can be your superpower.

CONCLUSION

Understanding and Magnifying the Impact

Community Movements and Their Relevance Today

This was a fantastic way to create conversation, community, and commerce centered around fantastic local food!
— MEGHAN JAMISON HUNT

I RECALL THE EARLY DAYS of the Takeout 25 phenomenon. Who would have thought that a community Facebook group would become the Pied Piper of takeout food? It quickly became a digital revolution, with people trading dinner ideas instead of political memes!

The idea was simple, or so it seemed at first. Each household was encouraged to spend a mere $25 a week on takeout dining during the height of the COVID pandemic. It was like a superhero mission—save the day by ordering your favorite comfort food! But what began as a small effort to support local restaurants soon evolved into something spectacular.

People got so creative with their orders! I believe I saw one post that said, "I ordered sushi, a burger, and tacos, all this week—I'm *having a food Olympics in my living room!" But Takeout 25 wasn't just about food; it was about community. Takeout 25 group became a hub for neighbors to share food recommendations and information about their own culinary escapades. It really made a difference, both for the restaurants who benefited and for the community as a whole, providing connection and purpose at a time when people really needed those things. Now Takeout 25 is expanding into sustainability efforts and green dining. There is still much that is left to be done.*

Who knows what wild foodie adventures await us next? One thing is for sure, in Oak Park, we are not just dining; we are dining with style, with laughter, and with a whole lot of heart.

—**ROB GUENTHNER**, President and Co-founder of Kettlestrings Restaurant Group, Takeout 25 board member, and OPRF Chamber of Commerce board president

On the face of it, Takeout 25 injected hope into a hopeless situation by making a small and specific ask of community members. Community members could see their small action directly contributing to the well-being of their community. It was also fun to share food experiences with community members to break the pandemic isolation. It was a welcome escape from the death and sickness all around.

Creating Grassroots Movements

The specificity of the ask, the excitement of a shared experience, food as an engaging point of connection, being part of a tangible solution, and contributing to a cause bigger than oneself were all factors that contributed to the grassroots movement that Takeout 25 became.

The steps to create a grassroot movements are:

- Clarify why people should come together.
- Start with a specific, achievable ask. Keep it simple.
- Connect people to a broader purpose/mission with the ask.
- Communicate consistently and fearlessly.
- Accept help without diluting the focus.
- Partner with other groups and networks to create scale (traditional media, social media groups, not-for-profits, and even entire communities).
- Promote engagement and make it fun.
- Be fair and positive.
- Lead from the front and be prepared to care and commit more than everyone else.

Harnessing a Movement

Creating a movement is one thing, but harnessing it to deliver long-term impact and value is a different thing altogether. That requires organizational constructs to create value and economic constructs to capture that value and distribute it among all the stakeholders.

Take a closer look at Takeout 25 and you will see that we created a micromarket aligned to the local community and encouraged community members to spend their disposable income into this micromarket in ways consistent with their values. Even if this shift in community spending patterns was a small percentage per household, it collectively translated to substantial dollars getting retained in the local economy supporting local small businesses.

Restaurant owners often get into the food business because they love cooking and feeding people. They may not all have the same level of business acumen or marketing skills. The Takeout 25 community, through its posts and comments, levels the playing field for restaurants in the Takeout 25 micromarket by providing distributed marketing support, as opposed to each restaurant centrally managing their respective marketing efforts. Takeout 25 also facilitates collaboration/cooperation between restaurants to create a resilient local economy. This allows restaurant owners to focus more on providing compelling dining experiences locally.

So the economic construct and its relevance and scalability was established. The long-term relevance was further bolstered by expanding the mission from the focus on economic empowerment of local food businesses to include food security and sustainability. These are two large topics that communities will grapple with for a long time to come. Equally important, we needed to create an organizational container to formalize our activities, and in our case, we chose the not-for-profit route to make sure that Takeout 25 aligns with the needs of the community and not with the interests of a few.

The steps to harness a grassroot movements are:

- Establish future relevance. Use the vision and mission to articulate why the group exists.

- Choose an organization type that fits your need (not-for-profit, LLC, S corp, C corp, etc.).
- Communicate the relevance of the organization to the community.
- Establish organization/team to pursue vision. Think creatively. (We used a volunteer-based model with internship support because we did not want to deal with payroll and other administrative overheads that came with that choice.)
- Convert the movement to a marketplace that allows you to distribute the value created equitably.
- Ensure balanced focus of demand side (community members), supply side (restaurants), and enablers (e.g., not-for-profits, partners).
- Create guiding principles for decision-making.
- Create a revenue mix that balances risk. (In our case, we started with donations and events, then we expanded to grants, merchandise, and residuals from consolidated services.)
- Leverage technology for efficiency.

Community Commerce

Takeout 25's core focus is food. Our efforts often spiral out to touch and enable other aspects of the local economy without diluting our core focus. We harness the power of community to enable the local economy.

I'm calling this *community commerce*.

TikTok defines community commerce as "creator-driven word-of-mouth marketing." Community commerce sits at the intersection of community, shopping, and entertainment. We are adding a few important elements to our definition of community commerce:

- The community in our definition is not just virtual communities on social media. Our social media community is the virtual manifestation of the physical communities we live and raise families in.

- Our positivity rule focuses on building inclusive and diverse communities while also maintaining a safe and cohesive space for community members and small businesses. It creates and maintains productive positivity within a large group.

- The community's shared values are a consistent focus in our activities. This will be different in different communities. This focus is maintained through partnerships with impactful local nonprofits addressing social issues the community cares about. We use nonprofits as proxies for community values.

Hence, in our definition of community commerce, we mobilize a community virtually in a positive movement to shop consistent with community values. We encourage community members to share shopping experiences and insights in entertaining ways to support small businesses in a physical community by inspiring others.

Relevance in the Age of Amazon and Uber

We live in the age of Amazon, Uber, Netflix, DoorDash, and others. These innovative, digitally enabled business models provide frictionless convenience in many facets of our everyday life. All our needs are delivered to our homes, packaged affordably with just a few easy clicks.

I am a proponent of the power of digital transformation and its promise for progress. In fact, I help organizations digitally transform by disrupting the status quo. So the perspective I share in this book is ironic. I believe these new digitally enabled models tend to extract money out of local communities, and many in our society have accepted this trend and its consequences as inevitable. Without viable alternatives, it's natural for people to feel that way.

The convenience we expect from these new models often comes at the expense of thriving local communities. It comes at the expense of local food and retail options that contribute to community building and livability. Local communities are important units of society, and people choose a city/town to live in based on their desire to be part of that community, its people, and its values. This sense of belonging is often fostered by the local activities available in communities, especially local food. Food represents the taste and diversity of a community. And the presence of a vibrant local food scene helps community members knit their community together by sharing time with each other and creating memories over a meal.

I do not believe the convenience that Amazon, Uber, and others deliver will or should go away anytime soon. However, I do believe that they can coexist with locally aligned models like Takeout 25 that help build thriving sustainable communities.

12

External Recognitions Helped Gauge Community Impact

Takeout 25 has made such a difference in our community. It has greatly helped restaurant owners. Story after story, we hear how it saved them. It helped residents discover new places, food, and drinks. It also created a community online and a place to bring us together even when we couldn't dine together. It has been a great experience sharing the love of local restaurants with each other. I wish every town had Takeout 25 groups. Oh, we were traveling in South Bend (Indiana) and found their Takeout 25 group and then because of that found the best restaurant to stop at on our road trip.

—TINA HARLE

AS THE PRESIDENT AND CEO of Visit Oak Park, I've always believed in the power of community. Our story of resilience during the COVID-19 pandemic, epitomized by Takeout 25, is a testament to this belief. This initiative was not just a lifeline for our cherished local restaurants; it was a beacon of hope and unity in our community.

When Ravi Parakkat proposed Takeout 25, it was clear that this was more than an economic strategy. It was a call to preserve the heart of our tourism economy: our local restaurants. These *establishments are not just eateries; they are storytellers of our community, offering a taste of Oak Park's rich culture and history to both residents and visitors alike.*

The response was overwhelming. The Takeout 25 Facebook group became a digital town square, where residents shared meals, stories, and support. This initiative brought to life the true spirit of Oak Park, showcasing the unity and strength of our community.

I witnessed firsthand the transformative impact of Takeout 25. Restaurants that had been on the brink began to see a resurgence. Furloughed staff returned to their roles, and the vibrancy of our local dining scene was rekindled. This movement wasn't just about survival; it was about reinvigorating the soul of our community.

Understanding the significance of this initiative, Visit Oak Park was proud to nominate Takeout 25 as a Silver Lining Story for the Illinois Governor's Conference on Travel & Tourism in 2021. The recognition it received, winning the award for Most Innovative Pandemic Startup, was a moment of pride for all of us. It highlighted not just the ingenuity of Takeout 25 but also the unyielding spirit of Oak Park.

As we move beyond the pandemic, Takeout 25 remains a symbol of our resilience and communal strength. It is a reminder that in times of crisis, the Oak Park community stands united, ready to support each other. This initiative has taught us the importance of sustained commitment to our local businesses, ensuring they don't just survive but thrive in the long-term.

In conclusion, Takeout 25 is more than an initiative; it's a legacy of our community's strength and unity. As we look to the future, it stands as a shining example of what we can achieve together, not just in crisis but in all seasons of life.

—**ERIC WAGNER**, CEO, Visit Oak Park

Awards

In January 2021, I was named a 2020 Villager of the Year by the local newspaper for the impact my initiative, Takeout 25, had on the community during the pandemic. This acknowledgement came as a surprise to me. People were still dying, and businesses were struggling, and the pandemic was showing no signs of receding. We were still very much in the midst of a pandemic, but it was an acknowledgement of the impact the idea was having in our community. It also provided more visibility and lent more credibility to our grassroots movement.

A few months later, Visit Oak Park, the state-certified convention and visitors bureau for western Cook County, recognized Takeout 25 with a hometown hero award. In addition to Oak Park, Visit Oak Park represents the communities of Bellwood, Berkeley, Berwyn, Broadview, Brookfield, Elmwood Park, Forest Park, Franklin Park, Hillside, La Grange, La Grange Park, Maywood, Melrose Park, Northlake, North Riverside, River Forest, River Grove, Riverside, Schiller Park, Westchester, and Western Springs.

That same year, Visit Oak Park also nominated Takeout 25 in the category of Silver Lining Stories: The Most Innovative Pandemic Startup at the Illinois Governor's Conference on Travel & Tourism.

We faced stiff competition in that category but ended up winning the award. Individually and together, these recognitions validated Takeout 25's success in its original mission of helping restaurants survive the pandemic. I was invited to the conference at Navy Pier in Chicago in December 2021 to receive the award. It was surreal to receive the award in the first place, and it was even more so to see the Takeout 25 logo up on the giant screen behind the main stage. Sitting there at the event watching the Takeout 25 logo stare back at me, the entire past year flashed in front of my eyes.

By the end of 2021, Takeout 25 was officially a not-for-profit with an expanded mission from economic empowerment of local small businesses to include sustainability and food security. In 2022, the local chamber of commerce recognized me as an Oak Park River Forest Community Titan for my contributions to the local small business economy. Later that year, the Village of Oak Park recognized Takeout 25's sustainability efforts with the OP Green Award. This built credibility for our sustainability efforts.

Case Study

In summer 2021, as I was setting up the not-for-profit, a chance conversation with my cousin, Dr. Bala Mulloth, who teaches social entrepreneurship, resulted in the Frank Batten School of Leadership and Public Policy at the University of Virginia (UVA) expressing interest in creating a case study on Takeout 25. The two-person team from UVA included assistant professor Dr. Bala Mulloth and graduate course assistant Arielle Watt. They spent the fall of 2021 interviewing a cross section of Takeout 25 stakeholders (community members, local political and economic development leaders, Takeout 25 board members, restaurant owners, and Takeout 25 moderators) and conducting primary research to collect and validate the details to build a case study.

Over the winter, they brought together their research into a comprehensive case study on social entrepreneurship featuring Takeout 25. The case study was titled *Takeout 25: A Community-Driven Entrepreneurial Initiative in Oak Park, Illinois*. It was released in January 2023 and is now available to academic institutions through Sage Publications. Through this case study, I wanted to share the Takeout 25 model with the next generation of business students and social entrepreneurs so they can build out the model to deliver an even bigger impact.

Community Reactions

However, the most important recognition for Takeout 25 was from the local restaurant owners, partners, and community members. Takeout 25 was created and continues to exist for and because of them.

Denise HairWiz Roy, Surf's Up
So thankful for not only the idea but also the effort to make it to TV, radio, print, T-shirts, and festivals. THE WORD IS OUT!!

Patrick O'Brien, Scratch Kitchen
Back up thirty-eight years, I'm a freshman at Fenwick High school (summer break). Mom wakes me (noon or so), takes me by the ear, and says, "You're not spending this summer at Oak Street Beach, young man!" Walks me up the block to the back door of Traveling Fare (gourmet caterer in River Forest). Says to the chef, "Put this kid to work!" I've never looked back! Thanks Mom! Opened my original location SKL in 2012, and that started my career as a

restaurant owner. Scratch On Lake, Scratch Deli, District Kitchen and Tap, Lathrop House Cafe, and Scratch Public House—some open, some have closed. The lessons I've learned through ownership and surviving a pandemic have taught me more about life and people than anything else. I often say I have to make this work because I can't do anything else, but TBT, I love this business and the people that exist within it and wouldn't change it for the world. TO25 has been a huge support to all of us. A huge thank-you to its originator, Ravi!

Sharadhish Chattopadhyay
Congratulations, Ravi Parakkat and the entire Takeout 25 team who worked tirelessly to help our local restaurants wade through the COVID-19 times and continue to do so. I feel so proud to stay in this community, which can come together for a cause like this and just help each other. Well-deserved award to Takeout 25 and Oak Park community who made this a successful initiative through active participation.

Sundeepa Kaur Chugh
A brilliantly helpful idea . . . a deserved accolade! Congrats!

Elizabeth Martinson Goodman
Incredible. Great leadership and vision! Congrats!

Brian J. Flynn
Congratulations, Ravi. Our community has been well-served during the pandemic thanks to Takeout 25.

External Recognitions Helped Gauge Community Impact

Dave McGee
Well done, Ravi Parakkat and team. You should be proud of what you've achieved! Great cause and has encouraged us to consider local a lot more! Oak Park has an amazing selection.

Beryl Schnierow Greenberg
Many congratulations! A well-deserved acknowledgment for all you've done for our community. And a brilliant idea too!

Carol O'Connor Ford
Takeout 25 not only helped to preserve our family's time-honored faves but introduced us to places we may never have tried but for the reviews and shout-outs. Special props to Ravi for his altruism and leadership!

Sharon Wolf Newton
Such a great way to support our friends and neighbors in the community and discover some great new favorites.

Donna Oswald
Takeout 25 Inspired me to order out more than I ever had in the past. It also exposed me to different restaurants throughout town. Truly a brilliant idea during the dark days of the early COVID shutdowns.

Kate Klest Kaufman
Loved all the recommendations and being able to support local restaurants. Found new favorites and still use it as a resource!

THE TAKEOUT 25 EFFECT

Cathy Raschke
Takeout 25 made me feel good about our community during a very difficult time. It is still going strong, and I still try new restaurants based on posts I see in the Takeout 25 Facebook group.

Michelle Sukup Jackson
Takeout 25 introduced me to a lot more of our local restaurants during a time we weren't able to support them in person.

Gretchen Burch
Takeout 25 was a simple way for an individual to help make a difference during the height of the pandemic. And I found a few new favorite restaurants!

Bambi Alexander
We have loved all the positive interaction that the Takeout 25 page has generated. Not just restaurant recs but getting to know our community people and businesses. Even though so much online and remote this past year, this site has become a movement fostering connection.

Renita Yu
Not only did Takeout 25 have a huge impact on Oak Park restaurants, the goodwill and proactive spirit it created spread to many other communities both near and far. It was very helpful to have a place to go to find out which restaurants were struggling and for restaurants to promote new services like whole family meals as opposed to individual servings.

External Recognitions Helped Gauge Community Impact

Anne Perkins Lane
Takeout 25 was what Oak Park needed during the pandemic. Fantastic concept that is still helping local businesses today.

Lisa Peters
Takeout 25 was a life-changing group for me! I had just moved to the area less than six months before the lockdown, so I wasn't familiar with most of the local restaurants. This group saved me! I could see posts and reviews about all of our restaurants and even get recommendations on restaurants outside the area. Plus, I got to contribute to helping them stick around so that I could visit in person someday! I do my best to continue spending $25 weekly in this awesome neighborhood! Thank you!

Mechelle Wesley
Takeout 25 provided Oak Park residents the opportunity to support local small businesses in a way that was both safe and effective during a time of great uncertainty. The initiative provided much more than capital to businesses, also becoming a valued space for neighbors to engage, share, champion, inform, and encourage one another during the pandemic.

Michele Carr
Takeout 25 was a great resource for me since I moved to Oak Park just before the pandemic. It continues to be my go-to place learn about new restaurants or great experiences from local residents in the area. When I'm hungry but not sure where to order from, I always discover the perfect spot after reading Takeout 25 posts. And it feels great to support our local businesses at the same time.

THE TAKEOUT 25 EFFECT

Tammy Suski Barrett

This was such a brilliant idea! Saved our restaurants, got the community involved in something positive during a very dark time, and motivated residents to try restaurants they had never even heard of before!

Laura Berrios Best

So many great meals and inspiring comments and reviews thanks to Takeout 25 Oak Park. The group helped so many restaurants that continue to feed our great community.

Ana Garcia Doyle

Takeout 25 has had such a positive impact on my family and our community. At a time when folks felt (and are still feeling) isolated, Takeout 25 has helped us build community around supporting our incredible restaurants!

Greer Haseman

During the dark days of the pandemic/lockdown, many felt disconnected. Takeout 25 was not only a way to help local restaurants through this hardship but it allowed us in Oak Park to feel a connection to each other. A connection by helping our favorite restaurants, a connection by challenging us to try new ones. Even a connection through sharing photos of our meals at home. This connection during a time of struggle has strengthened our community and inspired others. It was like sharing a meal with all of Oak Park.

External Recognitions Helped Gauge Community Impact

Kim Frost
Takeout 25 has not only connected the community, it held us together. The feeling we get when supporting out local restaurants and sharing our likes and recommendations has brought so many of us closer together and led us to new and wonderful culinary experiences.

Joan Chiolak Petertil
Takeout 25 shined a light on our restaurants and their struggles during the pandemic. Wonderful idea to get residents supporting local restaurants more!

Jim Major
Outstanding concept. Extremely helpful to our wonderful restaurants and community as a whole.

Julie Johnson Zeller
The many Facebook posts on Takeout 25 Oak Park were so much fun to read. Much conversation about favorite menu items at restaurants across the village.

Bonnie Lewis Prokopowicz
A perfect example of how this group continues to help our community: a beloved local restaurant had a devastating fire yesterday. Ravi Parakkat has used the group as a means to consolidate support for the owner and employees, as well as other businesses nearby that were affected. Because this group has such wide reach, it is the perfect venue for expanding the community's ability to help this local gem of a restaurant in its time of need.

THE TAKEOUT 25 EFFECT

Alan Peres

Great effort to support all local restaurants during COVID. Didn't favor one over another. You choose where to spend your money— just spend. Also introduced consumers to places they may not have known about and got people talking with one another, building community.

Laurie Casey

When I discovered Takeout 25, I talked with my family, and they went all in. Pre-pandemic, we might have eaten restaurant food maybe once a month, but ordering takeout turned into a steady, once-a-week activity for my family.

Shannon Saliny

Takeout 25 has been the most exciting way to try new restaurants! I look forward to the pictures and recommendations daily, and it's helped me to visit many local places. The positivity of the group is refreshing!

Sara Yount

Takeout 25 is a wonderful marketing and community-building tool. It is a way to shine the spotlight on all of the wonderful restaurants in our community. We tried new dishes and new restaurants because of the raves and recommendations shared via Takeout 25.

Kyle Monk

Takeout 25 has rallied the community! Ravi and the Takeout 25 team continue to plan ways to engage and support the community even past the original mission of generating money for local restaurants during the worst of the pandemic.

External Recognitions Helped Gauge Community Impact

Kalliani Premachandran
A fantastic idea to help a local industry keep afloat amidst the hard pandemic days. Also to bring together the people of the community to help towards a noble cause. A big salute to Takeout 25 and to Ravi, the man behind this. All the best going forward.

Jennifer Chhatlani
Takeout 25 brought the community together on something super easy and simple that almost everyone can do—order food! It is a model for and testament to how anyone really can make an impact.

Aberdeen Marsh-Ozga
This was, and is, such a great initiative! Kudos to the organizers for highlighting the effort, craft, and love our restaurant and bakery owners put into their work. We Oak Park–area foodies are happy to participate (and to learn and try new things) as part of the Takeout 25 Oak Park community!

Alli Galecki
The photos and recommendations of everyone in this group completely shifted how I look at this industry as a whole. So thankful for the leadership, and I spent closer to $100 a week as a result and so happy to do so!

Nicole Donohue
Takeout 25 was such a great idea not only to help businesses survive but also to build community in a time when that was and is hard to do. With all the isolation and division we live with these days, it feels empowering to have a common goal.

THE TAKEOUT 25 EFFECT

Best of all, it is easy to support: Who doesn't want to have a reason to order great food? I love how much I have learned about new restaurants that haven't been on my radar before. It also helps develop a deep level of appreciation about what the restaurant owners and industry are dealing with right now. It is much easier to pay a little more and be patient waiting for your food a little longer than expected knowing the struggles and how hard everyone is trying.

Thank you for starting this program, Ravi, and for everyone who helped grow it.

Rajesh Nair

Amazing innovation that not only delivered much-needed employment locally but brought the community together. I am sure this one will inspire many more projects (tech + social).

Mary Bunn

To say that I love Takeout 25 Oak Park might be a bit of an understatement. I enjoy seeing so many people sharing their local food experiences and photos, and I have discovered so many great places in the process. We're lucky to have so many wonderful options.

Mary MacGregor

Takeout 25 is a terrific group! It opened up so many restaurants for us that we would not have tried without all the photos and reviews. Plus, we learned of so many places we didn't know about. It was a welcome lifeline to our community during the pandemic lockdown. Thanks to Ravi! It's a great idea and continues to grow and thrive.

External Recognitions Helped Gauge Community Impact

Rowen Glusman
Takeout 25 has been one of the most wholesome Facebook groups I've seen. The fact that so many people can be joined through their love of food and desire to help their community is fantastic!

Carol McMahon Shea
We've lived in Oak Park for twenty-three years, and the Takeout 25 community allowed us to share our family favorites and inspired us to branch out and find new favorites.

Charisse Burns
A light during a difficult time—and helped connect us to our neighbors!

Leslie Lauderdale
Takeout 25 helped our community to pull together in a time fraught with fear and isolation.

Mark Lukas
Simple, brilliant, and effective for all!

Yvette Birriel
We love Takeout 25! Not only are we helping community restaurants but also it opened our eyes to new places! We make it a point to support weekly! Something different!

Christine DuSell and Ron Elling
When Takeout 25 first debuted in the throes of the pandemic, we adopted its message and practice almost as a patriotic duty. But, in

addition to believing that we were truly helping the Oak Park restaurant industry survive, we looked forward to our takeout nights as a pleasant change from the humdrum of pandemic lockdowns. We've continued that tradition and still look forward to our (almost) weekly takeout nights of the delicious meals available here in Oak Park. We're glad and hope we contributed to the survival of so many fine establishments!

Sandra Sokol

Brilliant idea, during challenging times; helped save restaurants; helped people learn about the many eating establishments in and around Oak Park.

Afterword

IF YOU ARE CIVIC-MINDED, I hope what I've shared in this book makes it a little easier for you to find your purpose and pursue it. The last three years have been extremely rewarding for me, and they have opened up a wide range of possibilities—possibilities I never knew existed, possibilities that would never have opened up if I had stuck with the familiar and comfortable. It took me forty-four years to muster the courage to make the choices I made to seek and pursue my purpose.

It may look very different for you. You might choose to focus on a different social or economic need in your community. So regardless of your age, gender, race, location, financial situation, etc., seek your purpose and pursue it with dedication and passion. Do it in ways that help your fellow humans and contribute to the community you live in. That's a reward in itself!

Mobilizing your community to seek tangible solutions to shared problems will become increasingly important in our world. Each and every one of us can do it in ways big and small for the people around us. That said, it will not happen unless you decide to take that first step. I hope the template provided in this book helps you take that first step and guides you along the way. Don't wait for anyone or anything. Start now.

Today is the first day of the rest of your life.

—Charles Dederich

As for the Takeout 25 team, we will be focused on incubating new ideas to create community value. We will also be exploring opportunities to scale the overall model and successful ideas across communities. We plan to invest in technology that will help us scale the model while efficiently delivering more services and support to local restaurants.

To set up Takeout 25 in your community, please contact us at: takeout.25.op@gmail.com.

Acknowledgments

I STARTED ADDRESSING the members of the Takeout 25 Facebook group as "Dear Takeout 25 family" in my posts a couple of weeks after we launched Takeout 25 on November 17, 2020. Over the past three years, this family has grown. Together we have shared many ups and downs along the way. Without the community members and business owners stepping up and being a part of this family, Takeout 25 would not be what it is today. So to everyone who has been a part of our journey, thank you. I'm truly grateful.

Committed volunteers have been the backbone of the Takeout 25 movement. Their time and commitment have allowed us to pursue our mission. Early volunteers who stepped up to help set up the group, administrators and moderators who shaped the group's conversations, the volunteers who helped us plan and execute events, the Takeout 25 board, and several others have all contributed to this movement. Thank you. This would not have happened without you.

I want to specifically talk about three people (a community member, a moderator, and a local restaurant owner) who played important roles in the Takeout 25 story but are not with us anymore.

Carrie Banks, who was part of the creation of Takeout 25 Taste the Town event, passed away shortly after the first Taste the Town event. I was shocked and saddened by that. This total stranger had been moved by the Takeout 25 story to reach out and initiate Taste the Town, only to then tragically pass away that same year. This had a deep impact on me personally. This was the first time death played villain in the Takeout 25 story, but it wouldn't be the last. Thank you and rest in peace, Carrie!

John Trilik's knowledge of and passion for food, local restaurants, and Chicago food history were apparent the first time we met at Brewpoint Coffee in Oak Park. I brought him on as a moderator, and in a short period of time, he made a big impact on the group with a series of posts around his quests. Unfortunately, John passed away suddenly. He brought his personality and perspective to the group through his posts and left a lasting mark on the group during his short time with us. Thank you and rest in peace, John!

I have already shared the story of George's restaurant deciding to go against the indoor dining ban and how the ensuing community backlash prompted me to start Takeout 25. Now let me tell you about Donasaki Konstantos (Saki), who was the owner George's son and the one active on social media. Through the early stages of Takeout 25, I got to know Saki, and we developed a friendship. In his midthirties, Saki was quite the character and had an unforgettable personality. He was so full of life, but we tragically lost Saki in November 2021 exactly a year after Takeout 25 was formed. I was shocked and saddened by the news. I went to his funeral but could not find words to console the distraught family. Saki's death hit me hard and was the lowest point for me in the Takeout 25 journey. Thank you and rest in peace, Saki!

To all our partners (local nonprofits, community organizations, media outlets, sponsors, churches, restaurants, etc.) and

Acknowledgments

other service providers. Your willingness to partner with Takeout 25 at specific points in our evolution made a huge difference. You have all inspired me with your willingness to serve our community in impactful ways. We hope to build on our partnerships to pursue success for our community. Thank you.

To all our partners, volunteers, and community members who have contributed their stories to this book. The Takeout 25 story is your story, and I'm privileged to be sharing it with the world. I want to thank Bethany Brown DeCaspers for helping me understand and navigate the process of creating and publishing this book. I want to thank the people who helped review and edit the manuscript: my wife, Amy, and friends Paul Clark, Ravi Kiran, and Basab Bhattacharya. I also want to thank Fletcher Martin and John Harris from a5 Inc for the preliminary book cover design options.

Special thanks to Rishad Tobacowalla for always being available to share his wisdom as a successful author and for pointing me to Josh Bernoff's book *Build a Better Business Book*. Josh's book was a useful reference guide for me as I worked through the different stages of this book.

I have to acknowledge how important family support was for me as Takeout 25 was launched and through its evolution these past three years.

To my kids, Rowen and Reva. Takeout 25 has at times been a third child that has competed for my time and attention. Thanks for jumping in and helping support your sibling, and thanks for your patience as I was trying to figure things out. You both mean the world to me, and I love you very much. Thank you.

To my wife, Amy. She was the first one I shared the Takeout 25 idea with. She was the one who helped create the flyer for restaurant owners. She would take these flyers out on her walks and drop them off at local restaurants. She would chat with restaurant owners, patiently explaining the Takeout 25 concept. (She does that better than I ever could.) She is the one who reached out to NBC and Fox to see if they would be interested in the Takeout 25 story. Later in our evolution, she started managing events for Takeout 25. I want to thank her for being patient with me, challenging me as necessary, and forcing me to focus on family when I got too deeply involved with Takeout 25 and my other commitments. Needless to say, the Takeout 25 journey would be different without her involvement. Thank you, baby!

Last but not least, I want to thank my parents, Prasanna and Ramakrishnan, for raising me in a loving environment and providing me with the education and tools to pursue my purpose. Takeout 25 would not exist without them.

Resources

Takeout 25 Website: www.takeout25.org

Takeout 25 Oak Park Facebook Group: https://www.Facebook.com/groups/takeout25oakpark

Takeout25 Instagram: https://www.instagram.com/takeout25nfp

Takeout25 LinkedIn: https://www.linkedin.com/company/takeout-25-nfp/

Financial advisor referenced: Andrew Palomo, Pillar Financial Advisors

Takeout 25 UVA Case study link published by SAGE: https://sk.sagepub.com/cases/takeout-25-community-driven-entrepreneurial-initiative-in-illinois

***Chicago Tribune* article**
Takeout 25 Has Saved Local Restaurants in Oak Park. Now It's Flexing Its Spending Muscles across the Chicago Border, in Austin.

THE TAKEOUT 25 EFFECT

NBC 5 coverage
Oak Park Residents Pledging $25 a Week to Help Save Restaurants amid COVID Panic

Axion News
"Food as a Social Lubricant": Supporting Local Restaurants; Empowering Communities

WGN *Outside the Loop*
Takeout 25 Oak Park
Takeout 25 Expands
Takeout 25 Is Helping Keep Local Businesses Going during the Pandemic
Illinois's First Green Dining District
Takeout 25's Boxed Water
Illinois's First Green Dining Hub

***Wednesday Journal* Articles**
2020
Introducing: Takeout 25 Oak Park
The Takeout 25 Effect
Food Focused Villagers of the Year in 2020

2021
Takeout 25 Embraces Spirit of the Season
Taste the Town Take Two
Takeout 25 Expands to Austin
Taste the Town Savoring Success
A Symbol of Sustainability

Resources

Third Time Around for Taste the Town
Financial Success for Taste the Town 3 despite Service Hiccup
Takeout 25 to Launch as Nonprofit at Barrie Fest
Happy Crowd Munches through Barrie Fest, Courtesy of Takeout 25
Reinventing Nonprofits, Restaurants Team with Rush Warming Center

2022
Taste the Town: Putting the Pieces Together
Taste the Town – In Person at FitzGerald's
SEOPCO and Takeout 25 Bring a Food Focus to Barrie Fest
Takeout 25 Leading Local Green Dining Initiative
Takeout 25: Goodness and Gift Cards

2023
Takeout 25 Launches Boxed Water. A Bargain at 99 Cents.
Becoming Illinois's First "Green Dining Hub"
Barrie Fest Returns

About the Author

RAVI PARAKKAT IS A FERVENT ADVOCATE for a sustainably managed, digitally enabled future. Since becoming a US citizen in 2016, he transitioned from a corporate consulting career spanning three continents to a purpose-driven journey in public service. In recognition of his contributions to local small business driven economy during and after the pandemic, Ravi was honored as Oak Park and River Forest's Villager of the Year in 2020 and Community Titan in 2022.

He founded Takeout 25 in 2020, a pioneering initiative supporting local restaurants through the pandemic's challenges. This effort was recognized as the Most Innovative Pandemic Startup at the Illinois Governor's Conference of Travel and Tourism in 2021 and bagged the Oak Park Green Award in 2022.

On the political front, Ravi was elected to the seven-member Oak Park Village Board in 2021, amassing the highest votes. He joins his board colleagues to set and fund the policy priorities for Oak Park, Illinois, a community with fifty-five thousand residents and about $200 million in budget. In his trusteeship, Ravi prioritizes community safety, community affordability/fiscal discipline, and sustainable and equitable economic development. Ravi's civic dedication can also be traced back to his roles on the Oak Park Environment & Energy Commission and a private Waldorf school's board, which he guided to national recognition as a Green Ribbon School.

With engineering and business credentials, combined with vast business and board experience, Ravi currently serves as the vice president of digital transformation at Junior Achievement of Chicago. Here, he steers the nonprofit's embrace of digital tools to further their mission of empowering youth for success.

Over two decades in consulting, Ravi worked across industries from financial service and energy to manufacturing. His portfolio boasts partnerships with global brands during pivotal moments, including Ford Motor Company, Morton Salt, BP, Enbridge, Consolidated Edison (ConEd), and the Canadian banking industry during its post-2008 financial crash recovery. He's managed multimillion-dollar projects and consultancies focusing on technology-enabled transformation.

Originally from the picturesque state of Kerala, India, Ravi began his consulting career in 2000, relocating to the US in 2003. Now, he resides with his beloved family: wife, Amy, daughters Rowen and Reva, and their feline companion, Naveen.

Learn more at **www.raviparakkat.com**.

Printed in the USA
CPSIA information can be obtained
at www.ICGtesting.com
LVHW090103050424
776347LV00003B/11

9 798989 919512